He's Asked You Out...
Now What?

What will it take to find and keep a decent boyfriend?

Will you ever find someone nice enough and nuts enough to want to go out with you?

Once you have a boyfriend, how do you keep the relationship on the right track?

Is it possible to win the dating game and not lose your mind?

Now That He's Asked You Out:
Straight Talk for Girls

Now That You've Asked Her Out:
Straight Talk for Guys

Mom and Dad Don't Live Together Anymore:
Help and Encouragement
for You and Your Parents

Surviving the Tweenage Years:
A Guide for Parents and Youth Workers

Now That He's Asked You Out

GARY & ANGELA HUNT

Here's Life Publishers

First printing, October 1989
Second printing, June 1990

Published by
HERE'S LIFE PUBLISHERS, INC.
P. O. Box 1576
San Bernardino, CA 92402

Library of Congress Cataloging-in-Publication Data
Hunt, Gary.
    Now that he's asked you out : straight talk for girls / Gary and Angela Hunt.
    p.   cm.
    Summary: Uses a Christian perspective to discuss such aspects of dating as
standards, selection of companions and places to go, dating as a preparation for
marriage, and the issue of premarital sex.
    ISBN 0-89840-258-1
    1. Dating (Social customs) — Juvenile literature.   2. Dating (Social cus-
toms) — Religious aspects — Christianity — Juvenile literature.   3. Teenage girls —
United States — Religious life — Juvenile literature.   [1. Dating (Social
customs) — Religious aspects — Christianity.   2. Christian life.]   I. Hunt, Angela
Elwell, 1957 —   II. Title.
    HQ801.H945   1989
    646.7'7 — dc 19   89-30704
                                              CIP
                                              AC

Scripture quotations are from *The Holy Bible: New International Version,* © 1973, 1978, 1984 by the International Bible Society. Published by the Zondervan Bible Publishers.

In order to protect the privacy of certain individuals, all of the names in this book have been changed.

For More Information, Write:
L.I.F.E. — P.O. Box A399, Sydney South 2000, Australia
Campus Crusade for Christ of Canada — Box 300, Vancouver, B.C., V6C 2X3, Canada
Campus Crusade for Christ — Pearl Assurance House, 4 Temple Row, Birmingham, B2 5HG, England
Lay Institute for Evangelism — P.O. Box 8786, Auckland 3, New Zealand
Campus Crusade for Christ — P.O. Box 240, Raffles City Post Office, Singapore 9117
Great Commission Movement of Nigeria — P.O. Box 500, Jos, Plateau State Nigeria, West Africa
Campus Crusade for Christ International — Arrowhead Springs, San Bernardino, CA 92414, U.S.A.

We don't play with diamonds,
We don't trifle with gold,
Life's greatest treasures
We don't carelessly hold.
We prize them, extol them,
And cherish them so—
And love is the best gift
We'll ever know.

To our daughter, Taryn.

A Note to the Reader...

My husband and I have worked with young people like you for years.

In most of our counseling situations, we find that the teenagers we talk with are troubled about dating relationships. Why shouldn't they be? Everyone has a different opinion on the subject, and it's hard to tell who's right and who's wrong anymore.

In this sexually active and explicit age, someone needs to do some "plain talking" to young people.

We've searched the Bible, our own personal experiences and the wisdom of others to bring you a healthy and balanced view of sex. We're not living in the past; we know how many kids today are sexually active and think it's no big deal.

But sex *is* a big deal, and in its proper place and time it can be a tremendous pleasure and source of closeness for you and your loved one. Read this book carefully and think and pray about what you learn.

We wish God's best for you.

—Angie

Contents

1

Love Makes
the World
Go 'Round,
But What Exactly
Is It?

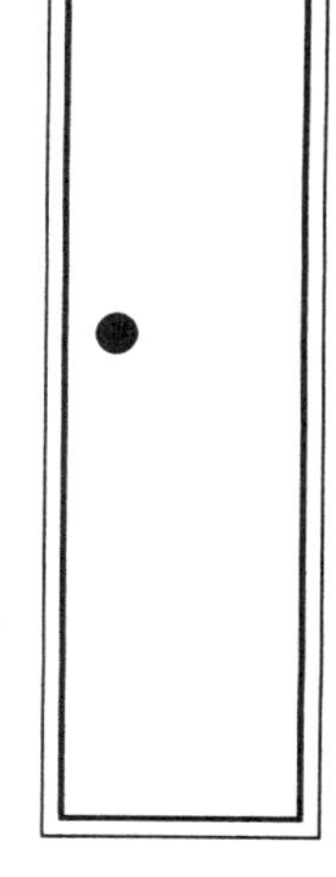

You're walking into school on a chilly winter morning. You pass your fellow students as they gather in small groups around the lockers and outside the restrooms.

"Hey, man, that's great!" a football jock tells his buddy. "You'll earn over a thousand bucks in one summer doin' practically nothin'. If only I could find a job like that."

You stop inside the restroom to check your makeup. Three girls are gathered around Melanie, one of the most popular girls in school.

"So what's he like?" one of the girls wants to know.

"Well," Melanie purrs, "let's just say he's close to the best I've ever had."

"Where'd you do it?" another girl wants to know.

Melanie throws back her head and laughs. "In my own room. My parents had gone to church and I told them I was going shopping with a friend." She pauses and flutters her lashes. "I think I'm in love again."

As you pass the teacher's lounge, you overhear the health teacher talking about his lessons: "And I'm supposed to teach today where the cervix is and how to insert a diaphragm! Next week it's AIDS education and the week after that it's nocturnal emissions and menstruation. I can't believe I'm teaching this stuff. By the way," he pauses, blowing smoke out of the corner of his mouth, "any of you seen those brochures about the confidential abortion services? I'm supposed to hand them out to the freshmen today."

Tom and Joyce, one of the hottest couples on campus, are locked in a lingering farewell kiss outside the door of your first period class. Her hands are in his jean pockets and his run up and down over her body as they kiss.

You slide into your seat and sigh. The world your parents knew (*How'd it go today, honey? Have you found a nice boy to like?*) is gone forever and somehow this world doesn't look kindly on girls who walk through the halls unattached.

What will it take to find and keep a decent boyfriend? Will you ever find someone nice enough and nuts enough to marry you? Can you play this "dating game" without either being a prude or breaking all of your parents' rules? Will you ever find real, lasting love?

Falling In Love

I remember so clearly the first time I felt the zing of love! I was in the fifth grade, and I had just seen an attractive, strong, noble, courageous, heroic young man on television. He was wonderful! In the course of a half hour, I watched him save a damsel in distress, battle wickedness and remain absolutely gorgeous through it all!

When the television show was over, I sat upside down in my favorite chair to have a good think. *You're being silly,* I told myself. *Not only are you in love with a television hero, the guy is not even real — he's a cartoon!*

That's what first love is all about — excitement. It doesn't have to be practical or even realistic, and it has nothing to do with sex. It only has to feel like L-O-V-E!

My first love lasted for about a day, but I never forgot my cartoon hero or the warm wonderful feeling of caring for someone.

When did you first feel your heart go pitter-patter over some guy? Maybe your first love wasn't practical or realistic, either, but it sure felt wonderful, didn't it? Even though one minute you're as high as you can be and the next minute you're in the pits of depression, the adventure of being in love is a wonderful experience.

Love Is...

What is love? We say we love sports cars, new clothes and McDonald's French fries. We love God, we love our parents and, although on some days you may not like to admit it, you love your brothers and/or sisters. But in each case our love is different. My love for crispy French fries doesn't come close to the love I have for my dog. And the love I have for my dog isn't nearly what I feel for my family.

The Greek language, which was used to write the New Testament, has three words for the one word we English-speaking people call *love*. The first word is *phileo* which refers to a "brotherly love." The love you have for your good friends is one example. The second word for love is *eros* which refers to a sexual love. Our word *erotic,* meaning "tending to arouse sexual desire," is derived from *eros*.

The third Greek word for love is *agape*. This word is used to refer to the pure and unending love God has for you and me. This *agape* love, described in 1 Corinthians 13, is not selfish, demanding, rude, insensitive or jealous. It is love in the best sense. It is the love I hope you will find someday when you are married.

Love Isn't...

But how does love develop from an initial attraction and "pitter-patter" to *agape* love?

Well, first let's talk about how it *doesn't* develop.

When you watch TV and movies or listen to songs on the radio you may think you're getting a pretty good idea of what love is about. After all, most shows and almost all songs deal with either falling in love, being in love or giving up love. To be honest (and I've been in love for quite some time), they don't give you the whole picture.

I used to get a kick out of watching that old show *The Love Boat* on television. In a seven-day cruise, a man and a woman would meet, flirt, fall in love, fight, break up, make up and get back together just in time to walk off the ship and live happily ever after. Neat, huh?

Well, in real life things don't usually work that way. There are lots of couples who fall in love quickly, marry quickly and divorce quickly. But that isn't real love. *Real* love has staying power.

In a recent, popular movie, two guys were sort of in love with the same woman. Aaron, who was a little on the nerdy side, was Jane's truest friend and confidante. They understood each other better than anyone else possibly could. Then Tom entered the scene and his good looks and likeable personality got poor Jane all in a muddle. After

Tom kissed her and stroked her under a moonlit sky, Jane was ready to jump into bed with him.

The movie had a logical ending because neither guy ended up with the girl. Jane's relationship with Aaron was just friendship; her relationship with Tom was totally physical. True and lasting love requires more.

Love is *not* the stuff you hear rock musicians sing about either. Jon Bon Jovi admitted as much in an interview: "It's hard to believe that the majority of teens today are so shallow minded. Our songs are about lust, not love."[1] Vulgar descriptions of the sex act distort the beauty of the loving relationship God wants *you* to enjoy someday with one man.

How Love Grows

Just as there are three kinds of love (*phileo, eros* and *agape*), there are three stages to love:

	When we say:	**We mean:**
Stage 1: **Friendship**	"I love you."	"I like being with you as a friend."
Stage 2: **Affection**	"I love you."	"I like being with you more than I like being with anyone else. I have great affection for you."
Stage 3: **Lasting Love**	"I love you."	"I will spend my entire life with you no matter what happens."

When I was sixteen I fell in love with a young man I'll call Jim. He was older than I, a dynamic leader in our church youth group and a fine Christian. I could see no wrong in him, and after a few dates I was ready to say the three little big words: "I love you."

He loved me too, and we continued dating steadily. We grew to know each other better and then he asked me to marry him. "I love you," he said, and of course I answered, "I love you too. I'll marry you."

We planned our wedding in secret because I knew my parents would have a fit if they found out I was engaged at sixteen.

On my seventeenth birthday we decided to make our engagement public. After all, we were mature young people, almost adults, so we announced to my parents that we intended to be married.

What a mistake! My birthday party was ruined. My mother was obviously upset; Dad retreated in silence; only Jim and I were left to pretend to be festive.

Over and over I reminded my mother that she had married at seventeen, so surely it was all right for me to get engaged now and marry Jim when I would be eighteen. Jim was a fine Christian — what could she possibly have against our marriage?

"Jim is a fine young man," she told me, "but he is not right for you."

I shrugged off her objection, but underneath I felt a nagging worry. If my parents wouldn't and couldn't approve of my marriage to Jim, I didn't know if I could go through with it. All my life I had been taught that children are to love, respect and obey their parents. Leaving home to marry a young man my parents didn't approve of didn't seem to fit that description.

After a few months I realized I could not take the final step and promise to spend my entire life with Jim. I broke off our engagement and immediately a huge weight was lifted off my shoulders. The relief I felt made it clear to me that my feelings for Jim weren't enough to sustain a marriage.

I realize now that in my relationship with Jim I was only in Stage Two: I had deep affection for him. I could not commit myself to Stage Three: love throughout life no matter what.

The three different stages of love involve the three different parts that make up a person: the intellect, the emotions and the will.

	The part:	**What it means:**
Stage 1: **Friendship**	Intellect	"I'm getting to know you, and I like what I see in you."
Stage 2: **Affection**	Emotions	"I like you so much that I am happy when you're with me and lonely when you are not. You are becoming very important to me."
Stage 3: **Lasting Love**	The Will	"I want you to become precious to me. I will love you even when my intellect and emotions tell me not to."

You see, love at levels one and two can be broken off because affection and friendship are based upon knowing someone and being with someone. Love at Stage Three is based upon commitment. You say, "I will love" and your love remains strong when your guy is away, when he makes you angry or upset, and when you discover his character faults. Stage Three is the love you will promise to give when you take your marriage vows. You will swear to love, honor and cherish till death parts the two of you.

Lasting Love

Let's do a little mental exercise. Take a moment to think of the person you would most like to love for the rest of your life. Perhaps you already have someone in mind; perhaps your "dream guy" is someone you haven't met. Picture now a romantic courtship, flowers, happy times, sunny picnics in the park, quiet nights and gentle kisses — you've got the idea! Now picture a beautiful wedding with candles and your friends all dressed up in taffeta gowns and watching proudly. Don't forget the romantic honeymoon!

Now imagine the day after your tenth anniversary. There are a couple of kids running through the house and your dream man has gained twenty pounds and lost his hair. Last week you spent too much on clothes for the kids so there's no money for this week's groceries. Your hubby enters the room and says, "I wish you'd learn to manage money better. No matter how much we earn, there never seems to be enough for all the things we need and want."

Where is your love now? Even when your husband is no longer a mystery and you know everything about him (including his annoying habits), and even though emotionally your heart no longer leaps when he enters the room, lasting love is the undercurrent that binds families together.

Lasting love lets you know someone is always there to care about you. If you have lasting love, you can work through the difficulties. Lasting love takes time to develop and time to maintain. It doesn't head for the divorce court whenever trouble arises. And you shouldn't be ready to commit to it until you're *really* ready to get married.

God is the best example we have of *genuine* lasting love. He loves us even though He knows us better than anyone else could ever know us. He knows the ugly things we keep hidden from the rest of the world and He still wants to be our best friend.

God has great affection for you too. He gives you good and perfect gifts such as the food you eat and the gorgeous world you live in. He is grieved when you are away from Him and comforted when you are in His will.

God's love is complete and perfect. He loves you with His intellect, His emotions and His will. Even when you were far away from Him in sin, He loved you enough to give the best He had to give: His son, Jesus Christ. Christ loved you enough to commit to die so that you might live. He didn't want to die. His human body cried out against the pain He knew was coming. But He did it for you. His commitment to love was that strong.

When it all boils down to simple facts, love equals commitment. Are you committed to Christ? Are you ready to be committed to love?

Think About It...

1. Do most couples who date say, "I love you" too soon? What do most teenagers really mean when they say, "I love you"?

2. What is the difference between an initial attraction to someone and lasting love?

3. Think about the three stages of love (friendship, affection and lasting love). At what point in a dating relationship should each stage be entered?

4. Could you ever love someone as much as God loves you?

2

Why Set Dating Standards?

Samantha liked Randy the first time she saw him. He had an outgoing personality, a perfect smile and a build that was terrific.

She couldn't believe it when he asked her out! She spent hours picking out clothes and makeup and fixing her hair. They joined a bunch of their friends for a night at the movies.

Their date was going along great—she was saying the right things and he seemed to be enjoying himself—until the gang gathered outside the theater after the movie. Someone suggest they all go to the park for some "fun." The girls looked shyly at each other and the guys laughed.

Samantha knew what kinds of things went on in the park. She also knew what kind of hassling she'd get if she didn't go. She looked at Randy, but he seemed to be leaving the decision up to her. She wasn't sure what to do . . .

Have you ever found yourself in a situation like Samantha's? If not, I'm sure you will.

One of the purposes of this book is to give you guidelines for setting personal standards so you'll know what to do when you have a tough choice to make. But before we start making specific standards, we need to know *what* standards are and *why* they should be set. Why not just "go with the flow" on a date and have a good time? Why not get some birth control pills from your doctor or the school clinic just in case things should ever go too far? Why worry about rules and regulations? Things are different today, aren't they? Standards are for goody two-shoes.

What Is a Standard?

Yes, things are different today, but no, standards are not just for Wally and Beaver Cleaver. A standard is a guideline for behavior, or a rule. Your teachers set standards for classroom behavior, otherwise every day would be total chaos. Your parents set standards for their work, otherwise they may find themselves out of a job. You've set standards for yourself, even if you never really thought about it like that. Have you decided that you won't cheat on a test? That's a standard. Perhaps you believe it's wrong to lie. That's a standard too.

Since standards protect you from potentially harmful situations, doesn't it make sense to have standards where your dating life is concerned? For some reason I'll never understand, most guys expect girls to set the standards and draw the line. Guys should have standards too, but most of them will simply go along with the ground rules a girl sets. So you can see why it's important for *you* to have your standards clearly set in your mind.

Many girls just assume they will have sex before

marriage. I've watched a lot of popular TV shows where the mother or father sat down with their son or daughter and said, "When the time is right for sex, you'll know it. Don't rush it." I've *never* heard a TV parent set the standard, "Sex was made for marriage. Hold off until then and you'll never regret it."

Why Set Standards?

My husband and I designed a poll on sex and dating and gave it to thirty-five teenagers from our church youth group, ages fourteen to eighteen. Every student who answered the poll said they had a personal relationship with Jesus Christ.

One question on our poll was, "Is being a virgin before marriage important to you?" Eighty-five percent said yes, although 60 percent admitted being a virgin wasn't important to most kids.

Why is being a virgin important? According to those we polled:

"You should be a virgin because of God and diseases," one girl wrote. "But unsaved people don't think twice about sex before marriage."

"It is very important to me," wrote another young lady, "because God says it is wrong to defile your body." But she admitted she had another reason: "With so many diseases around, sex scares me."

A sixteen-year-old girl said being a virgin wasn't important to her. "It depends on if you are really in love," she said, "and if you have been together for a very long time and know each other very well. Everybody is doing it."

Is virginity important to guys? "Yes," said one fifteen-year-old guy, "because once you lose it you cannot ever have it again."

"My dad would disown me," admitted a fourteen-year-old, "and I do feel that it is right to wait for marriage."

"You don't have to worry about getting a girl pregnant," wrote a young man.

Not every Christian guy we interviewed wants to keep his virginity. "I don't think the girl I marry would mind if I wasn't a virgin," said a fourteen-year-old. "And I want to know what sex feels like."

So why do Christians set the standard that sex is for marriage and marriage alone? The poll said:

"So you don't get diseases," wrote a girl, "and so you can save your virginity for your wedding night."

"So you will only have sex with one person and it will be special for the first time."

"Because God made sex for married people to use as a way of reproduction."

"AIDS."

"Because it is an act of love between a man and his wife and not something to do just because it feels good."

When asked, "Why do Christians believe we should abstain from sex before marriage," 60 percent of our young people replied, "Because God (or the Bible) says so!" but 70 percent of the group couldn't think of a single place in the Bible where it says we should not have premarital sex!

What God Says About Dating Standards

According to the answers to our poll, everyone had a different standard! And most weren't based on what God *really* has to say. If you say you're against premarital sex just because you've *heard* it is wrong, and a tough choice comes along, what is to stop you from throwing what you've heard people say out the door? Has "what people say" ever stopped you before? As Christians, we ought to look to God first as our standard setter.

And if you really believe the Bible forbids premarital sex, shouldn't you know *where* the teaching is found? Let's take a look.

The Bible does teach that premarital sex is wrong, but there is not a single verse that says, "Thou shalt not have sex before marriage." A lot of the kids who took our poll listed the "Ten Commandments" as the Bible's teaching against sex before marriage, but the Ten Commandments forbid adultery, not premarital sex.

The Bible tells us that our bodies were made by God, they bear God's image (Genesis 9:6 and Colossians 3:10), and they are wonderfully made (Psalm 139:14). In 1 Corinthians 6:18-20, the Bible specifically tells us why we should set standards and guard our bodies:

> Flee from sexual immorality. All other sins a man commits are outside his body, but he who sins sexually sins against his own body. Do you not know that your body is a temple of the Holy Spirit, who is in you, whom you have received from God? You are not your own; you were bought at a price. Therefore honor God with your body.

The day you gave your life to Christ, the Holy Spirit came to live within you. Your body is not your own; it is the temple of the Holy Spirit. In order to honor God with our bodies, we should keep ourselves morally pure throughout our entire lives, fleeing from all sexual sins including premarital sex, homosexuality, adultery and lust:

> It is God's will that you should be holy; that you

should avoid sexual immorality; that each of you should learn to control his own body in a way that is holy and honorable, not in passionate lust like the heathen who do not know God. For God did not call us to be impure, but to live a holy life (1 Thessalonians 4:3-5,7).

See that no one is sexually immoral, or is godless like Esau, who for a single meal sold his inheritance rights as the oldest son (Hebrews 12:16).

Do you remember the story of Esau and Jacob? Esau was very, *very* hungry and Jacob had a good-looking bowl of stew. For a simple momentary physical pleasure, Esau gave Jacob something he could never retrieve—his larger share of the family inheritance, his birthright as the oldest son.

Don't give in to the temptation of sexual impurity just for a simple momentary physical pleasure or a temporary relationship. You will be giving up something you can never retrieve—the precious gift of your virginity, something which ought to belong to the man you will someday marry.

More Reasons to Set Standards

Not only should you remain morally pure in obedience to God, you should also remain pure out of respect for your parents and for yourself. Respect yourself enough to know you don't have to sleep with a guy in order to be worthy of his love. And although your parents may seem to burden you with rules about curfew and questions about where you are going and with whom, they are only concerned for your safety.

Unfortunately, many parents expect their kids to remain pure without giving instruction in the areas that really count. Did your folks call you in for a heart-to-heart chat, blush and say, "Just don't ever go all the way, okay?" Did they tell you *why* you should keep yourself morally pure? Perhaps they gave you a detailed lesson on menstruation, birth control and the reproductive cycle, but they didn't tell you how far is too far.

Maybe they simply handed you this book! If so, let them know you want to discuss the ideas presented at the end of each chapter.

The final reason to set standards is probably the most important.

Remember the three parts of love and the human being? There are also corresponding levels of physical involvement. Total physical intimacy, or sexual intercourse, belongs to those who have committed themselves to lasting love at the marriage altar. That is the way love works best and that is the way God intended it to be.

Stage 1: **Friendship**	Intellect	Little physical involvement
Stage 2: **Affection**	Emotions	Increased physical involvement
Stage 3: **Lasting Love**	The Will	Total physical involvement

God knows the heartache which can result from immorality. Immorality is sin, and the Bible tells us that sin brings death: "After desire [lust] has conceived, it gives birth to sin; and sin, when it is full-grown, gives birth to death" (James 1:15).

God knew about AIDS before scientists ever diagnosed the disease. He knows about the heartbreak of divorce. He knows how frightened a pregnant teenage girl can be. He cares deeply when an unborn baby is killed before it is given a chance to live. He also wants to protect you from all of this.

How to Set Your Standards

When you were small you lived by your parents' standards. Now that you are a teenager, you live by a combination of standards — some of your own and some of your parents.' When you are an adult, you will live by your standards alone. So practice setting your own standards now.

How do you set standards? The most important advice you will need comes from the one who created the human race in the beginning, God Himself. His guidelines and standards are written in the Bible. If you follow the wisdom contained in the Bible's pages, you will be assured of a rich and full life in the will of God.

I'll never forget the excitement of signing up for Driver's Education. I was finally going to be able to drive! But before I could drive, I had to sit through hours of classroom teaching, watch horribly realistic films of automobile wrecks, study the driver's manual and spend time behind the wheel with my instructor's foot constantly in reach of the spare brake pedal.

Once I passed my driver's ed class, I had to go down to the Florida State Licensing Bureau and take a written and a driving test. I didn't think I was ever going to get my mother's big car parallel parked! But I did, and on my written test I correctly answered questions about highway safety, traffic signs and safe braking distances.

I had to understand the rules before the state of Florida would let me drive! Now, as a seasoned driver, I have to continue to obey the rules or the police department will take my license away. If I obey the laws, driving is fun and I do not pose a danger to other people on the road.

Your dating life is a lot like driving. Before you begin to date, you should learn about what rules to follow, know what could happen if you disobey those rules and decide in your heart that you are going to behave responsibly and correctly toward God and man. If you goof up, you not only hurt yourself, you hurt your entire family and other people who may be watching your testimony.

One of the biggest disagreements teenagers have with their parents is the battle over *when* the teenager will be allowed to date. Some girls begin dating at eleven and twelve; others aren't allowed to date until they are sixteen.

Our poll indicated that most teenagers think sixteen is the best age for beginning "single dates in a car." But chronological age isn't really important. What *is* important is your maturity, responsibility and willingness to understand and obey your own dating standards.

You are old enough to date when you can write down a list of standards which are acceptable to you *and* your parents and *agree to abide by them no matter what happens.* Your standards should be guidelines which will allow you to honor the Lord in any given circumstance. Your standards will insure your safety and assure your parents that you will behave responsibly.

In Ephesians, Paul wrote:

> Children, obey your parents in the Lord, for this is right. Honor your father and mother—which is the first commandment with a promise—that it may go well with you and that you may enjoy long life on the earth (Ephesians 6:1).

Would you make out in the back seat of a car if your

mother were along on the date? I doubt it! If you want your parents to trust you, your behavior on a date should always be parent-approvable.

When Standards Aren't Kept...

By now I hope you see the importance of setting God- and parent-approved standards and sticking to them. Two friends of mine didn't follow through on their standards and it changed their lives permanently.

Someone very close to me, I'll call her Joy, became pregnant while unmarried. Her Christian family was shocked and thrown into total confusion and deep turmoil. A marriage was hastily arranged, and though the young man professed to be a Christian, the marriage ended in divorce shortly after the birth of the baby. Now Joy and her ex-husband constantly argue over custody rights and visitation schedules.

Was it God's perfect plan that Joy become pregnant? No. Can Joy be forgiven? Yes. She has asked forgiveness of God and her family. Can good come out of her situation? Yes. The Bible says if we love Him and seek His will, good can result from our sinful mistakes. Joy has been forgiven and has made her peace with God, but she now lives with the consequences of her sin. She loves her son (he's a delightful child), but the struggle with her ex-husband may continue for years.

I met Diana when she was in seventh grade. I had the joy of leading her to Jesus Christ one summer at youth camp, and we spent hours talking together. When she left our junior high Sunday school department, I didn't see Diana very much, but she often called me just to keep in touch.

One day she called and said she had a boyfriend.

"That's great," I teased, "but you be careful and remember not to do anything God wouldn't want you to do. I'll be very upset if you ever get pregnant." I knew Diana had two older unmarried sisters at home who were raising babies.

Over the next few months, Diana called often to say that she and her mother weren't getting along. Finally she quit calling.

I saw her nearly a year later. She came to our church gymnasium where she knew I'd be. She was desperate to tell me something, but she couldn't find the words. I took a quick guess. "You're pregnant, aren't you?"

She nodded and her eyes filled with tears. "Will you ever speak to me again?" she wanted to know.

I sat down on the bleachers next to her and put an arm around her shoulders. "Of course, honey. I'll always be your friend. But I never want to see this again," I said, taking a gooey snack cake out of her hand. "If you want to have a healthy baby, you can't eat Twinkies for dinner!"

I advised her to make peace with her mother and go home, but Diana moved in with her boyfriend's family. After she had her baby, her boyfriend left for two years to do a stint in the Army. Diana is a young mother tied down at home, living with her boyfriend's family and still unmarried. She jumped from a bad situation into a worse one. I can only hope and pray that she will seek the Lord and make the right decisions.

Someone cares about you and doesn't want you to end up in a situation like Diana's or Joy's. Take a moment right now and tell the Lord that you are going to implement a set of standards to provide protection and guidance throughout your dating years.

Think About It...

1. Why should you set dating standards?

2. Are these standards to be unbreakable? Why or why not?

3. How old should a girl be before dating? What things should be considered before a girl begins to date?

4. What if a girl's friends are all dating, and her parents won't let her date? What are her options?

5. It has been said that Romeo and Juliet were only fourteen when they fell in love, and many Bible scholars think Mary, the mother of Jesus, was only thirteen or fourteen when the Savior was born. Why don't people marry today at thirteen and fourteen? How have times changed, and how should dating practices be changed to reflect today's society?

6. Why do Christians believe we should abstain from sex before marriage? What Scripture(s) support that belief?

7. Is being a virgin before marriage important to your friends? Why or why not? Is it important to you?

Setting Your Standards

At the end of the next few chapters, we've listed some standards for you to consider setting for yourself. If you're ready to make the standard a part of your life, put a checkmark in the box.

Your first three standards are simple:

☐ I agree that I am old enough to date when my parents and I can agree on a written set of standards.

☐ I agree to abide by those standards throughout my dating life.

☐ I know that details such as curfew, off-limits locations, etc., are to be set by my parents and may change as I grow older.

3

Date Saints

Two girls huddled together and talked about the boys in their class. A Sadie Hawkins picnic was being thrown by their church and, as humiliating as it was, the girls felt they had to ask someone to go with them.

"You could ask Bill," Julie volunteered.

"No, I couldn't," answered Susan. "He's not the type to even go inside a church."

"Well, he may never get inside a church unless someone like you asks him!" said Julie.

"Well, this is one time I'm not going to ask," replied Susan. "I don't believe in 'missionary dating.'"

"Okay, then," said Julie, chewing thoughtfully on the end of her pencil. "That leaves Charles, Scott, Jody and an assortment of guys I wouldn't be caught dead with."

Susan grinned. "Charles is Jewish, and Scott and Jody are from different denominations. I don't know if any of them would even want to come to our church."

"Well, it's up to you, of course," replied Julie airily. "But the picnic is in two days. You had better make up your mind."

Yes, Susan needs to make up her mind. But the issue here concerns more than one simple date. Susan and Julie need to decide what spiritual standards they will set for their entire dating lives.

Susan has already incorporated one important principle into her date life already. She doesn't believe in "missionary dating"—when a Christian young person dates a non-Christian young person in the hope that the non-Christian can be led to the Lord. Although I have seen one or two situations where an unsaved person did receive Christ as Savior, those cases were definitely exceptions. Most "missionary dating" simply does not work.

In the poll we gave our church young people, 40 percent said they would date a non-Christian; 35 percent said they wouldn't; and 25 percent said they "might." Of those who said they would, a surprising number said, "I could bring him to Christ," or "It would be a good chance to share the gospel."

"Sure, I'd date a non-Christian," wrote one guy, "if she was a good-lookin' babe."

"At this age I could change him," wrote a girl.

"I wouldn't date a non-Christian because I would become like her," wrote a wise fifteen-year-old.

"I wouldn't want to get emotionally tied up with a non-Christian because I'd have to break it off eventually," wrote a sixteen-year-old.

"I wouldn't mind dating a non-Christian," wrote another girl, "because some unsaved guys are as nice as Christians and I don't think we should shut them out."

One seventeen-year-old guy, who admitted he plans to lose his virginity before marriage, said he'd date non-Christian girls because they are more likely to "go all the way."

What Does God Think?

The Bible does not come out and say, "Thou shalt not date a non-Christian," but it does tell us that couples should not be "unequally yoked together":

> Do not be yoked together with unbelievers. For what do righteousness and wickedness have in common? Or what fellowship can light have with darkness? . . . What does a believer have in common with an unbeliever? What agreement is there between the temple of God and idols? For we are the temple of the living God. As God has said: "I will live with them and walk among them, and I will be their God, and they will be my people" (2 Corinthians 6:14-16).

"Oh, my boyfriend isn't a Christian, but he doesn't mind that I am," you may say. He may even attend church with you. But if he doesn't have the Spirit of Christ within him, you will never totally understand each other.

Vicki, a Christian girl from a great family, dated Shane all through high school and, quite simply, fell madly in love with him. Although he wasn't a Christian, his family was upstanding in the community and Vicki thought she could have a successful marriage. She and Shane married as soon as she graduated from high school.

For over three years they were relatively happy, but there were dark days. When Shane went out drinking with his friends, Vicki would wake up late at night to find her handsome husband vomiting over the toilet. Vicki endured bitter disagreements with her in-laws who couldn't understand her religious upbringing or her convictions.

"Can two walk together, except they be agreed?" asks Amos (Amos 3:3). Can two people walk joyfully together unless they serve the same Master? How can you develop a deep and totally understanding love if the person you are dating cannot understand spiritual things?

Non-Christians don't look at things the same way Christians do. If you are involved with an unsaved person in a dating relationship, it's important to realize you can never have the complete and honest relationship God desires for you to have.

If you want to know if it is God's will for you to date the guy you are dating, you must ask this question: Is he a Christian? If he is not, he is *definitely* not God's choice for you.

Can't Judge a Book by Its Cover

You should also consider whether you want to date someone who claims to be a Christian, but doesn't act like one.

Just because a guy is "religious" doesn't mean he is a Christian. And just because he attends a Christian church and says he is a Christian doesn't mean he has a genuine relationship with Jesus Christ. Paul had this to say in 1 Corinthians 5:9-11:

> I have written you in my letter not to associate with sexually immoral people — not at all meaning the people of this world who are immoral, or the greedy and swindlers, or idolaters. In that case you would have to leave this world. But now I am writing you that you must

not associate with anyone who calls himself a brother [a
Christian] but is sexually immoral or greedy, an idolater
or a slanderer, a drunkard or a swindler. With such a man
do not even eat.

From this passage we see that it is far worse to be
associating with someone who says he is a Christian but is
not, than with someone who doesn't claim to be a Christian
at all.

Paul is saying it is okay to be a casual friend of sin-
ners (could you have any friends at school if you weren't?),
but we should not even be casual acquaintances with someone who claims to be something he or she is not.

By the way, the word *associate* in those verses
doesn't mean *date*. Dating is a much deeper relationship
than casual friendship. Stick to being friends with guys who
don't know the Lord, and avoid at all costs any guy who
gives a good testimony in Sunday school and then tries to
get you to sleep with him on Friday night.

Joy, the young woman I mentioned in the last chapter, began to date Tom even though she wasn't sure he was
a Christian. They worked together and, naturally, they
began to spend time together.

Tom agreed to go to church with Joy, but the more
time she spent with Tom, the less time she spent in her own
personal devotions. Soon Bible reading and prayer just
didn't seem important. Tom began to push her to do things
she knew were wrong, but not until she knew she was pregnant did Joy realize what a mistake she had made.

Joy and Tom visited Joy's pastor for counseling. Ordinarily the pastor would never have encouraged a
Christian woman to marry an unsaved man, but when he
asked Tom if he knew Christ, Tom replied, "Sure. I'm a
Christian."

Joy and Tom were married; within a year they were divorced. During their short marriage, Tom beat Joy and frequently got drunk. They fought constantly. Tom told Joy he thought her church and her religion were nothing but stupid nonsense. The arrival of the baby only added to the problem.

Joy had never intended to marry a man who did not know Christ, but because she dated someone who wasn't living up to his Christian profession, she married a man who could not even love her as she should have been loved. God is love, and only those who know Him can love as He does.

How About Just One Date?

But suppose you know a really nice guy at school who may not be a Christian. You'd really like to go out with him, but you'd feel dumb going up to him and asking, "Are you a Christian?"

School does not always provide the opportunity to find out about another person's spiritual life. Sometimes only a one-on-one encounter will do it. So wouldn't one date with a guy who might not be a Christian be okay?

It all depends on what type of date you are talking about. There are different kinds of dates—group dates, double dates, single dates, serious dates, casual dates and dates purely for friendship and companionship. Maybe you have a best friend of the opposite sex, but you have no romantic interest in him whatsoever. Going out with him for a Coke doesn't feel like a date at all!

If you say you will *never*, under any circumstance, go out with a non-Christian, you may be isolating yourself from people too much. Let's say Joshua was invited by Joey to your church's youth activity. After the activity, you and your best friend want to go out for a Coke with Josh and Joey. You know Joey, and Josh seems like a nice guy, but what if Josh isn't a Christian? Would such a date be against your standards?

I recommend that you not date non-Christian guys on single dates or prearranged double dates. "Every date is a potential mate," my youth pastor used to tease. It's true! You never know when you are going to meet someone who will become a friend, a lover and a mate. So confine your dating of non-Christians to casual group dates. Who knows? Perhaps the combined testimony of you and your friends could be instrumental in leading someone to the Lord!

I wish I had set my standard in this area sooner. I once met a "nice" young man who worked in the building next to where I worked. After a casual introductory conversation, he asked if we could do something after work that evening. Thinking he was harmless, I said, "Sure."

After work we met and got into his car. His first question was, "Well, do you want to start off at a bar?"

I was thunderstruck. I didn't drink and wasn't even of legal age, so I laughed and said, "No. I think we've made a mistake. How old are you anyway?"

He was twenty-seven; I was seventeen. As we sat in the car he pointed to a gold wedding band which was hanging on his keychain. "I keep that there to remind me of a mistake I once made," he said.

I was horrified. "I think you'd better take me home," I told him gently. "You see, I'm a Christian. I don't drink. I'm only seventeen. And I don't go out with older divorced men."

After telling me about his many problems, he did

take me home. He called me several times during the following week, but I refused to see him again, although I did refer him to my pastor for counseling. I later learned he had lied about being divorced—he had a wife and two kids waiting for him at home.

After a few months, I saw him again. His picture flashed across the six o'clock news. He had come home from work and shot his family to death.

I was incredibly naive and stupid, and I'm not proud of that little episode from my personal history. But if it will help you to avoid an encounter with an innocent-looking person who could be dangerous, it was worth the telling. If I had formulated a set of spiritual standards and *stuck to them*, I could have avoided a potentially harmful situation.

You may not spend a lot of time thinking about the guy you will marry. If you are planning to go to college, you will meet—and date—a lot of new guys. If you are serious about a career, you will probably not marry until after you have earned your degree and found a job. The dating you do now will most likely be "friendship" dating—so keep it light, have fun and avoid heavy commitments!

One last thing to think about: Should you date people of another faith? Many people are devout believers of religions which do not accept Jesus Christ as the Son of God and man's only hope for salvation. Could a relationship with such a person honor the Lord? No. What if the relationship led to marriage? You'd each be going in different directions spiritually. We've already seen how harmful that can be for a marriage.

If you set standards for dating Christians and non-Christians, and stick to them, you may avoid a lot of heartache. Matthew 6:33 says, "Seek first his kingdom and his righteousness." Be sure the guys you date do so too.

Think About It...

1. Would you date a non-Christian? Why or why not?

2. What are the pros and cons of "missionary dating"?

3. Can a non-Christian guy truly understand a Christian girl?

4. Should you date a guy who says he is a Christian but is not acting like one? Why or why not?

5. If a Christian woman were to marry a non-Christian man, what sort of problems might they have in their marriage?

6. Suppose there is a guy at school who is nice and fun to be with, but you don't know if he is a Christian. What could you do to find out about his beliefs?

7. How can appearances be deceiving?

Setting Your Standards

☐ I will go on single dates only with Christians — those who are genuinely seeking after the Lord Jesus Christ.

☐ I will date non-Christians only in a casual group setting.

☐ I will go on single dates only with Christian guys who agree with my belief regarding salvation.

☐ I will never date a near-stranger.

4

How's His Social Life?

Once I fell hard for a young man I'll call Cal. Cal was shorter than me. He wore scruffy clothes, not because they were in style, but because he didn't own anything. And he *always* had this sweet dazed expression on his face. His family was scattered: His mother was divorced, and he hadn't seen his father in years.

We never actually dated, because I don't think Cal even knew what you were supposed to do on a date. Life to Cal was going to college, working and going to the beach.

Our lifestyles were worlds apart, but still we were attracted to each other and became good friends at school. Cal wasn't a Christian, but he was receptive to the gospel and always listened intently when I talked with him about salvation.

I really had a thing for Cal! I suppose it was my maternal instinct—something inside me just wanted to wrap him in a big bear hug and say, "It's okay. You'll be all right if I'm here to protect you."

A relationship with Cal would never have worked. We had nothing in common. But my feelings were so strong, if anyone had said anything against him, I would have risen to his defense, hissing and striking like a rattlesnake.

What kind of guy are you attracted to? Is he one of those brainy types your parents would approve of? Maybe he's a football jock or a long and lean basketball player. Perhaps you're attracted to the class clown, who is flamboyant and witty. Or do you prefer the quiet, "boy next door" type?

Perhaps you've been attracted to someone who isn't in the accepted stream of things. You know who I mean—the guy who is always in trouble with teachers or the law. Someone you *wouldn't* want to bring home to meet your parents. Sometimes it's easy to fall for these guys, because no one ever understands them until you come along.

Have you ever been infatuated with someone simply because he was a mystery to you? That mysterious feeling can be fun to explore!

If you begin to have deep feelings for someone quite unlike yourself, put your heart on hold and take some time to think. A person's background influences a relationship far more than you might realize. That's why you need to set social standards.

What? Does your date have to belong to a country club or something? No, that's not what I mean at all. There are just some basic things you need to take into consideration.

Opposites Attract?

At first glance, there are no two people on earth more different than my husband and I.

<table>
<tr><td>

Gary is:
- athletic
- an extrovert
- slow to make decisions
- a Beach Boys fan
- hyperactive
- quick-tempered
- a lover of adventure movies
- not a reader
- a cat lover
- from northern Ohio

</td><td>

I am:
- a klutz
- an introvert
- impulsive
- a Mozart lover
- slow and calm
- one who holds anger in
- a lover of romantic dramas
- a constant reader
- a dog lover
- from southern Florida

</td></tr>
</table>

We are an unusual combination. He watches sports on television for hours, but just the roar of the crowd gives me a headache. We are as opposite as two people can be.

But where it counts, we are very much alike.

<table>
<tr><td>

Gary:
- is a Christian
- is committed to the Lord
- is committed to our family
- is dedicated to his work
- doesn't care about being rich
- is easygoing
- loves kids
- is committed to me

</td><td>

I:
- am a Christian
- am committed to the Lord
- am committed to our family
- am dedicated to my work
- don't care about being rich
- am easygoing
- love kids
- am committed to him

</td></tr>
</table>

"Variety is the spice of life," they say, and "Opposites attract." These things are true. In fact, if it weren't for our differences, our marriage would be boring! I couldn't stand to live with someone exactly like me. My husband's differences make life exciting because we challenge each other to do things we wouldn't ordinarily do.

But our basic beliefs, the beliefs upon which we have built our marriage, our home and our family, are the same. If we disagreed about the basic principles of life, we could never agree to build a home and a marriage filled with love.

So if your boyfriend likes pepperoni on his pizza and you prefer sausage, don't give up! Those little differences keep a relationship interesting. But if your boyfriend is an atheist and you believe all things were created and are held together by God, your relationship is on dangerous ground.

Nothing in Common?

There are other things to consider when you are setting social standards. Not only should you date guys with similar backgrounds and beliefs, you should consider dating guys who like to do the same things you do.

If your idea of a nice date is dinner and a movie, think twice about going out with a guy who's into dirt biking. But don't be afraid to try something new! I must admit, one of the most interesting dates I ever had was with Bruce. Bruce was a real outdoorsman (I'm not really the outdoor type), and he took me out in his airboat to go gigging for frogs. We spent the better part of an evening in the swamp with alligators, mosquitoes and startled frogs who ended up on the end of a spear after we stabbed them from the airboat. That date was definitely different, but at least now I can say I've been gigging.

As long as a date is something your parents could approve of, you really don't have to be very concerned about trying something new.

If, however, the date includes alcohol and drugs, or being around other people who are doing alcohol or drugs, you should cancel the date. If you're already out on the date and you find yourself in this situation, *tell your date you want to go home immediately*. Look for an alternate activity where you won't have to compromise your standards.

In high school I was best friends with Karen, the girl across the street. Karen came to church with me and became a Christian, but her home life offered her no support and she never really grew in the Christian life. I liked her and tried to be a good influence.

One of the biggest fights I ever had with my parents concerned something really very simple. Karen had invited me to ride with her and some of her other friends to a football game. I didn't know her other friends very well, but I (and my parents) knew that these friends of Karen's were into drinking and drugs.

"Karen is my friend," I told my mother. "And just because some of her friends smoke and drink doesn't mean I'm going to! You just don't trust me, and I've never given you any reason not to!"

My parents were firm, although I stormed and cried and was insulted that they didn't trust me, their "responsible" daughter. They refused to allow me to ride with that group to the football game.

Looking back now, I'm sure I would have been uncomfortable if I had gone with them. I doubt I would have begun to smoke, drink or do drugs because of them, but just hanging around them would have been miserable. I'm glad my parents made the decision they did.

If you have decided to keep your body pure because it is the temple of the Holy Spirit, you will want to set standards about the types of dates you accept. There will be places and situations you should avoid.

What is the best way to stay away from questionable situations and places? Make sure your dates are planned.

Beware of the young man who calls you up and says, "I'll be over at seven to get you and we'll just cruise around." Cruise around doing what? Many kids get into serious trouble during the hours of undefined "cruising." If a guy cares enough for you to want to take you out, he should care enough to plan something special. The date doesn't have to be expensive or elaborate, but it should be planned.

If you are dating an unimaginative guy, try to plan some dates yourself. Come up with a variety of ideas for dates, because if you are really serious about someone you will want to see how they act in a variety of situations. Can your date handle a formal restaurant? Could he be patient if you took your younger brother or sister on a picnic? How does he feel about church activities? Could he take an otherwise dull afternoon and help you come up with some good, old-fashioned fun?

Remember—when you're thinking about a potential date, ask yourself these three questions:

    1. Why am I attracted to him?

    2. What do we have in common?

    3. What kinds of things would we both enjoy doing on a date?

Discovering and enjoying the differences and similarities between you and your date is half the fun of going out!

Think About It...

1. Why do so many girls fall for "rebels"?

2. Could a poor girl be happy dating a rich guy? Could a rich

girl be happy dating a poor guy?

3. Tom is from a Christian home, but his parents don't drink or smoke. Sally is from a Christian home too, but she and her family see nothing wrong with either smoking or drinking. Do you think this could cause problems if Tom and Sally dated? Why or why not?

4. Why is it easy to become infatuated with someone you could never love enough to marry? What is the difference between infatuation and love?

Setting Your Standards

☐ I will not seriously date a person with a drastically different family background.

☐ I will not knowingly date a person who engages in activities contrary to God's Word.

☐ If I am on a date and my date begins to use harmful substances, I will ask to be taken home immediately.

☐ I will not accept a date unless something specific has been planned. If the guy does not suggest a plan for the date, I will suggest an idea.

5

Romeo, Romeo, Where Are You Going to Take Me?

It was pretty late when Chuck pulled into Michelle's driveway at the end of their date. As he walked her up to the door of her house, they laughed, recounting their miniature golf game that had ended with Michelle's ball flying into a pond.

"It doesn't look like your parents are home yet," Chuck said as Michelle unlocked the deadbolt. "Mind if I come in for a while?"

He took her hand and smiled.

Michelle hesitated in the doorway . . .

Like spiritual and social standards, you need to consider physical standards in your date life.

"Physical standards? Don't tell me my date has to measure up in his looks too!"

Looks Aren't Everything

No. These physical standards have nothing to do with how cute your date must be. Your boyfriend may be blond, brunette, red-haired, black-haired or bald. He may be short, tall, thin, dumpy, stocky or frumpy. He may be a star athlete or the whisper-thin intelligent type who doesn't even know where the gym is. His looks are not important.

The Bible says that man looks on the outward appearance, but God looks upon the inward man (1 Samuel 16:7). When you are considering which guys you could date, don't be overly concerned about outward appearances. They can be deceiving.

Have you ever read *Cyrano de Bergerac* by Edmond Rostand? Cyrano was a wonderful, witty, charming man, but he had one problem — an incredibly enormous and ugly nose. He deeply loved an intelligent and beautiful girl named Roxanne, but Roxanne was infatuated with a handsome (but dull) young man named Christian. Roxanne would never have truly loved Christian (he was *really* dull), except one evening Christian stood below her balcony window and spoke eloquently of love. His words, his wit and his understanding, combined with his good looks, proved him to be a man she really could love, and she married him within ten minutes.

But unknown to Roxanne, the man who had really spoken those words of love in the semi-darkness was Cyrano.

Immediately after Roxanne and Christian were married, Cyrano and Christian were called away to war. During the weeks Roxanne and Christian were apart, they wrote long, passionate love letters, but Christian's letters were written by Cyrano, who lovingly poured out *his* real feelings to Roxanne.

Finally, unable to restrain her desire to see her love, Roxanne traveled to the battle site. But just after she arrived, Christian was wounded and he died in her arms.

For fifteen years Roxanne and Cyrano remained close friends. Finally, as Cyrano lay dying from a head injury evil men had inflicted upon him, Roxanne finally realized that the only man who could speak as did the man under her balcony was not Christian, but Cyrano. "I never loved but one man in my life," says Roxanne as Cyrano is dying in her arms, "and I have lost him—twice."

It's a sad story but it illustrates a simple truth: People are not always what they look like on the outside. So don't be so snobby that you won't consider a date with a guy your friends have labeled "gross" or a "geek." You may be pleasantly surprised.

After all, many of the best-looking guys in your school may be so stuck on themselves that they are no fun at all. If the best-looking guy in school acts interested in you, don't ignore all your standards!

So what if he is not a Christian, you might think. It is only for one date and he is absolutely the most gorgeous hunk I know! My friends would all die to be in my shoes. Remember, looks aren't everything. Sticking to your standards is far more important.

Where Are You Going?

Now let's consider the physical standard of *where* your date takes place.

When I was small my family and I often piled into our old station wagon and went to the drive-in on family night. We kids would usually go to sleep before the movies were over, but it was fun family entertainment.

When I was dating, however, my parents vetoed the drive-in as a place to go on a date. "We just don't want you going there," my mom explained. "It is not because we don't trust you, but there are other people who might not understand if they saw you coming out of a drive-in."

There are some places you should not go on a date because being seen at those places could harm your Christian testimony. Some of these standards will be determined by your parents, your church and the community in which you live.

How about your city? Are there places that could hurt your testimony if you are seen there with a date? Perhaps you live in a small city, and the "worst" place in town is a pool hall. Video arcades are bad news in some areas, but in others they are fun family entertainment. Maybe the quiet, pretty city park in your town turns into "Make-Out Manor" after dark.

You're probably thinking, *Why should I care what other people think of me? What does it matter? They shouldn't judge me anyway.*

I wish I could say it doesn't matter, but it does. Teachers, neighbors, friends and parents judge your character after noticing the company you keep and the places you go — that's just a fact of life. And people can and do judge your actions. The Bible says even a tree is judged according to its fruits.

"A good name is more desirable than great riches; to be esteemed is better than silver or gold," the Bible tells us (Proverbs 22:1). Whether we like it or not, Christians carry the reputation of Christ with us wherever we go. You are beginning now to build the reputation which will follow you throughout life. Take care to build a good one.

It's wise to ask this question when considering accepting a date: "Will my testimony be hurt if I am seen coming out of here?" You could also ask your parents. They will have a pretty reliable feeling for acceptable and unacceptable places for dates.

My mom and dad always told me what places were off limits. There were obvious places, of course, like bars and nightclubs, but there were some other places too. "Bedrooms are not appropriate places for dates," Mom told me, "and neither is a parked car. If you two are finished with an evening's activity and it is still early, bring your date home. I'll keep a supply of frozen pizza and Coke on hand."

The amount of business my sisters and I gave my mom's kitchen could rival that of our town's Pizza Hut. If our plans finished early, we'd simply suggest, "Want to go to my house for a Coke and some pizza?"

Think twice about *where* your date will be taking you. You'll probably avoid potentially awkward situations . . . and you'll give your parents peace of mind!

Spending Time Together

Let's be realistic. If you have been dating a young man for a long time, you'll want to spend more and more time together, but you can't go out every night of the week! Restaurants, theaters and concerts all cost money, and your boyfriend probably doesn't have an endless allowance. Where can you go without spending a fortune?

Most girls just invite their boyfriends over to study or watch television. That's fine, as long as he is out of the house by an agreed-upon time and you two are not alone in the house—appearances, remember? If you have your boyfriend over while your folks are out, you're inviting two things—temptation and speculation. Just make it a rule that at least one parent must be home (and awake!) before your boyfriend comes in the house, whether it's at the beginning of your date, your plans for the entire evening, or at the end of the date.

Would it embarrass you to invite your date to your home? Which would be embarrassing—the people inside the house or your house itself?

Shirley would die before she'd bring her date home because she knows her dad will be passed out on the couch with a pile of beer bottles beside him. Maxie hates to bring her dates home because her family is poor and their house is in a run-down section of town. Cindy will never bring any guys home because her family teases her unmercifully every time she has a boyfriend. Amanda doesn't mind bringing her dates home, but with her six brothers and sisters hanging around, she feels like the center of a three-ring circus!

If you feel you can't bring your date home (if the situation is beyond cleaning up or a good heart-to-heart talk with your family), then find another safe and inexpensive place to spend time with your boyfriend. Perhaps you can spend time in quiet conversation at the library, at a shopping mall or walking through a neighborhood park. Just avoid the parked car and empty house!

Time To Go Home!

What about *curfew?* Some parents set them; others don't. Some girls appreciate them; others can't stand to be told what time to come home.

I was in the tenth grade when I went on my first date with a football player. His name was Glen, and after he asked me out, I carefully explained our plans to my parents. I was going to ride to the football game with some friends, watch Glen play, wait for him to shower, and go out for a hamburger with him after the game. I told my folks I thought I'd be home by midnight. They approved.

But my calculations were way off. The game began at eight, was over at 10:30, and Glen wasn't finished showering until 11:00. We went to the local restaurant where *everyone* else went after the game, and we weren't seated until midnight. We ordered and didn't get our food until 12:30. Needless to say, I didn't get home until almost two in the morning.

Glen and I had a great time, but about two minutes after he pulled into my driveway, the front porch light flew on and my mother stepped out *waving a broom!* She was furious, and after ordering me into the house, she ordered Glen away. I was mortified. After trying to explain things, I realized I could have made everything a lot simpler if I had done one thing: called home.

My mom later apologized to Glen for behaving like a madwoman, but I learned an unforgettable lesson: If I were going to be late, I would call home. There was no need to worry my parents to death when a simple phone call would explain where I was and why I had been held up.

From that point on, I asked my dates where we were going. In the next breath, I'd ask my folks what time they wanted me back in. My parents and I would calculate about how long it would take and we would agree on a time to be back home.

Here's another idea that makes sense: If your parents tell you to be in at a certain time but they don't want to wait up, have them set an alarm clock for your curfew time. If you come in on time, you can turn the alarm off. But if the alarm rings, you're late and in hot water!

Something most girls never think about is the guy's curfew. Most guys are too proud to admit they have a curfew, preferring instead simply to take the heat if they come home late. Why not let your date know your curfew upfront and ask if he also has to be home at a certain time. Make it no big deal. You've probably been given plenty of time to have fun, so don't ruin the evening by complaining about your curfews!

If your parents (or your date's parents) give you a curfew, just be glad they care enough to want you home, safe and sound. Whether you live in a quiet little town or a bustling big city, there are normal-looking people who could and would hurt you if given half a chance. Don't blame your parents for worrying. Believe it or not, there will be times you'll be glad you can truthfully say, "Let's go. I have to be home in fifteen minutes."

Physical standards are important. If you set good standards and keep them, you will guard both your personal safety and your reputation.

Think About It...

1. Is it fair to "judge a book by its cover"? What character attributes can you judge by appearance? What things cannot be judged by appearance?

2. Joan and Don are out of the school concert at ten o'clock and Joan doesn't have to be home until eleven. Don doesn't offer any suggestions, so Joan feels like she should suggest something. What are her options?

3. Think of places in your town which are considered "shady." Now think of someone you admire very much as a Christian. What would you think if you saw this person

coming out of a "shady" place? How would it influence your opinion of him or her?

4. When people think of you, do they think of Christ? Why or why not?

Setting Your Standards

☐ I will *not* judge a guy's personality by his physical appearance.

☐ My parents and I will discuss and agree upon what places are not suitable for dates, and I will not go to those places.

☐ My parents and I will set a curfew before each date, based upon my age and the plans for the evening. I agree to call my parents and have my date call his parents if something unexpected comes up, and I agree to come home immediately if either set of parents ask us to.

☐ I will not park in front of my house for more than five minutes. If my date is not ready to leave, and the evening is still early, I will invite him in.

☐ I agree never to have a date inside my house unless at least one of my parents is home and awake.

☐ I agree never to lie to my parents about where I have been.

☐ I will work with my parents to help provide a suitable atmosphere at home in case I do want to invite a date over.

6

Teddie Too-Tight
or
Skimpy Sue?

Flirty Gertie is her name,
To other girls she's quite a pain.
She primps and scrimps and sways her hips,
When a guy's around, she puckers her lips.
The town's worst flirts rolled into one—
Flirty Gertie wants to have fun!

When Bertha Bosom comes into view,
Fathers blush and boys turn blue.
"If you've got it, flaunt it," is her motto,
But she flaunts it more than she really ought to.
Too-tight sweaters cut down to there—
Bertha's bosom needs some air!

Laurie Long Legs is quite a sight,
Loves to stretch her legs, all right.
In too-short shorts or skimpy dress,
Laurie thinks her legs are best!
Shaved and smooth, most every day
Laurie's legs are on display.

When Molly Makeup turned fifteen,
She realized her fondest dream.
"You can wear makeup," her mother said,
But Molly's freedom went to her head!
She paints her face, her eyes, her toes,
You can see her coming, way down the road!

Teddie Too-Tight crams herself
In clothes too tiny for an elf.
She buys outfits which are size seven,
When, truth be told, she wears an eleven.
Although her tight clothes make grownups frown,
Teddie doesn't mind — if she could only sit down!

Mindy Midriff is hardly a glutton
And she loves to show off her belly button!
Even in the cool winter air
Mindy's belly loves to go bare!
It's just a fad, and she's no dummy,
What's the harm in showing your tummy?

Girls, did you know the way you dress can keep guys awake at night? Did you know that some Christian guys are tempted to lust and practice impure habits because of how you dress?

That's their problem, not mine, you may think. *Those guys just have dirty minds.*

No, it's not as simple as that. Men and women are designed by God *differently.* Women are sexually stimulated by *touch* — gentle kisses and tender embraces. Men are stimulated by *sight alone.* For a man, *seeing* sexual images is nearly as big a turn on as sex itself.

Imagine yourself sitting on the beach, and every guy who walked by stopped, gave you a warm and tender kiss, and then walked away. How would you feel? Wouldn't you be frustrated and nearly nuts after a while? Probably so. Now think about a guy sitting on a beach and every woman he sees is nearly naked. How do you think he feels? Wouldn't you think he'd be frustrated and nearly nuts after a while? Probably so.

I once attended an open and honest meeting about sex. The discussion leader asked the guys a frank question: "What parts of a woman's body turn you on?" The primary answer was breasts, followed by legs and the tummy/hip area.

It may seem incredible to you that guys can actually become physically aroused by seeing part of a woman's body, but it is a biological fact. Men can be aroused by women's bodies, and although they may not always act on their sexual urges, you may be provoking guys you know to lust.

Women who understand this and who are considerate of others' feelings dress and act *modestly*. Now there's a word that has taken a beating over the years. I bet the first image that came to your mind when you read that word was a woman dressed from her collarbone to her ankles in some dreary black dress. But modesty does not necessarily mean old and frumpy and out of it. Let's define modesty and then look at positive ways to dress and behave tastefully.

Modesty Is Not a Bad Word

What is modesty? Webster's Dictionary defines it as "propriety [doing what is proper] in dress, speech and conduct." Let's take a look at these areas.

Speech and Conduct

In Proverbs 5, Solomon tells his son to stay away

from the adulteress whose lips "drip honey, and her speech is smoother than oil."

In the seventh chapter of Proverbs, a foolish young man is caught by a prostitute who is "loud and defiant, with crafty intent." She pretends to be religious, but seduces the young man with smooth talk.

Obviously, words can be just as seductive as how you dress. And what about actions? There is nothing wrong with playful teasing and fun, but when the teasing takes on sexual connotations, it's time to stop. Just be careful that your "flirting" doesn't get carried away!

Dress

In 1 Timothy 2:9 we read, "I also want women to dress modestly, with decency and propriety, not with braided hair or gold or pearls or expensive clothes, but with good deeds, appropriate for women who profess to worship God."

Similar advice is given in 1 Peter 3:3-5: "Your beauty should not come from outward adornment, such as braided hair and the wearing of gold jewelry and fine clothes. Instead, it should be that of your inner self, the unfading beauty of a gentle and quiet spirit which is of great worth in God's sight. For this is the way the holy women of the past who put their hope in God used to make themselves beautiful."

First, let me make something clear: These verses are *not* saying it is wrong to braid your hair or wear jewelry. Rather, they are saying that our primary concern should be how we look on the *inside*, not what we wear on the outside. Our actions and attitudes are more important to God than what we are wearing.

I remember my first date with my husband very

well. I can remember almost everything we said and did, but I can't remember what I wore. Believe me, the lasting impressions you make on people will not have as much to do with your clothes as they will with your actions and your words.

So does that mean you have to go through life looking like Plain Jane? No way! Christian women should always look and feel their best. We represent the Savior and we don't have to look like dowdy cast-offs. Just because you're modest doesn't mean you can't look good.

In biblical times, women were forced to be modest. Most women wore veils to cover their faces and their long robes covered them from their shoulders to the ground.

Our society is not the first to flirt with revealing clothing, though. Some of the Elizabethan outfits (in the 1500s) were so low-cut in the front that I wonder how the women kept from falling out of them!

Your best guideline for deciding what to wear: Be sensible. Don't wear shorts that expose your buttocks when you bend over. Don't wear pants so tight that your panty lines show through. And don't wear see-through blouses. Sometimes just the hint of a part of a body (like what shows through on some blouses or what is revealed in some slit skirts) is more provocative to men than simply displaying what's underneath.

I don't care, you may think. *I'm going to wear what's in style, and if men think bad things, well, that's their problem. I've got the freedom to wear whatever I want.*

You may have the freedom to wear whatever you like, but have you taken a moment to think of what the Lord would want you to do? Consider what the apostle Paul wrote:

> Everything is *permissible* [allowable] for me, but not everything is *beneficial*. Everything is permissible, but I will not be mastered by anything. The body is not meant for sexual immorality, but for the Lord, and the Lord for the body (1 Corinthians 6:12,13).

Clearly, your body is not meant to be a tool of temptation.

If you have a question about whether something you want to wear is appropriate, don't ask your mother, ask your father. He thinks like a man (that's obvious), and he'll be able to give you a man's opinion. If you don't have a father, ask an older, responsible male adult.

Modesty doesn't have to be a drag. Looking good does not mean looking sexy. Make dressing tastefully and working on your inner beauty your first priorities. Guys will *still* find you attractive . . . and for the right reasons!

Think About It...

1. You're shopping for a new bathing suit. What kind of guidelines should you set in making your choice?

2. There's a popular female rock singer who has popularized wearing a style of dress which, frankly, is very sexy. Several girls at school have already begun to wear them. If everyone's doing it, is it necessarily right for you? Is there an acceptable compromise?

3. How can a young woman be immodest in her speech? In her actions?

4. Are good manners and thoughtfulness a part of modesty? Why or why not?

5. What are some ways you can work on your inner beauty? What really makes a woman attractive?

Setting Your Standards

☐ I will go through my closet and discard any item of clothing my father feels is immodest.

☐ I will dress modestly, taking particular care on dates.

☐ I will try to be aware of immodest actions or attitudes I may need to change.

☐ I will make it my priority to become beautiful on the inside.

7

The Ladder
of Passion

I just wanted to get [sex] over with. I was sick and tired of hearing about it. I just wanted to say I had done it and no big deal." — a seventeen-year-old girl in Illinois[1]

"Like a city whose walls are broken down is a man who lacks self-control" (Proverbs 25:28).

You had your eye on him for months, and finally he began to talk to you. From his eyes you could tell he considered you attractive, and you knew how he felt for sure the day he paused by your locker and put his arm around your shoulder. You tingled at his touch, and although you struggled to remain calm, you wanted to shout, "Hey, look at this! He really likes me!"

Those first touches grow from hand-holding to gentle kisses. I'll be the first to tell you that kissing your boyfriend is *fun!* Your friends will tell you that making out is expected; your little brother will tell you kissing is gross; and your parents will tell you physical contact is dangerous.

How Far Is Too Far?

Why is everyone so mixed up about kissing/physical contact/making out?

When I was a kid, I heard a television announcer say, "Even today, couples still meet, hold hands, kiss and fall in love." I asked my cousin (who was three years older and wiser), "Doesn't he have it wrong? Don't couples meet, fall in love, hold hands and *then* kiss?" I was thinking that love was the initial attraction you feel for a guy, but my cousin knew better, "No, he's got it right. You meet, hold hands, kiss, and *then* fall in love."

The idea of kissing someone I didn't love was sort of repulsive, but now I laugh because I certainly kissed a lot of guys I had no intention of loving forever.

Kissing, a sign of affection, is far removed from sexual intercourse, the ultimate act of love intended by God to be shared between a husband and his wife. But kissing *can* be the "warm-up exercise" for sexual intercourse.

Do you remember our three-part chart? There is an application for this chapter as well:

Stage 1: **Friendship** (Dating)	Mental	Friendly physical contact
Stage 2: **Affection** (Engagement)	Spiritual	Affectionate physical contact
Stage 3: **Lasting Love** (Marriage)	Physical	Total physical contact

When you begin to date a young man, you will get to know him *mentally.* You will find out what sort of person he is, what he likes to do and what his goals are.

If all progresses smoothly and the two of you feel you should spend your lives together, you agree to be married. During this engagement stage, you become more united *spiritually* as you seek to know why God brought you together, how you can help each other to grow spiritually and how your goals can be united for God's glory in the future.

After you are married you become one *physically* through sexual intercourse. During the months and years ahead you will comfort, encourage and enjoy each other mentally, spiritually and physically. God's ideal plan results in more joy and fulfillment than you can possibly realize.

I like the way Dr. James Dobson describes sexual intercourse:

> Intercourse . . . is the name given to the act that takes place when a man and a woman remove all their clothing (usually done in bed) and the man's sex organ (his penis) becomes very hard and straight. He puts his penis into the vagina of the woman while lying between her legs. They move around, in and out, until they both have a kind of tingly feeling which lasts for a minute or two. It's a very satisfying experience which husbands and wives do regularly. They do it to express love for each other and because they enjoy it. In this way they satisfy each other. This is a fun part of marriage and something that makes a husband and wife very special to each other. This is an act which they save just for each other.[2]

Sexual intercourse is a natural and good part of God's plan for marriage. But few people today have the patience to wait for God's ideal plan. On television, in the movies and in music we are constantly urged to live simply for the minute. If sexual pleasure is within reach, we are told, grab it while we can. God's plan is unimportant, the world tells us, so forget His rules and do whatever you want, whenever you want to.

The rise of teenage pregnancy and the frequency of teenage abortions indicate that thousands of teenagers are grabbing for anything they think is love. Going to bed with someone is not love; it is not even an indication of true affection. Love involves spending time with someone, placing his interests above your own, and wanting more than anything to help that person find his personal fulfillment and joy in Christ.

If your physical contact with your date is heading toward sexual intercourse, you've gone too far.

Take the Initiative

You've probably heard from parents, teachers and church people that having sexual intercourse before marriage is wrong. I heard that too, and often! But no one ever took the time to tell me how far I could — or should — go.

For some reason I'll never understand, most guys expect girls to set the limits on physical contact. Well then, girls, set your limits and stick to them! I realize that's easier said than done, but consider this interpretation of 1 Corinthians 13 next time you feel a guy pressuring you:

> Though I tell you "I love you" and quote the words from the most romantic rock song I know, if I'm only doing it so you'll make love to me, my declarations of love are worthless.
>
> And though I tell you I'm the only one who understands you and really loves you, if I ask you to sleep with me, my words are worth nothing.

And though I give you gifts and bring you flowers and write you poetry, if I expect you to go all the way or become involved with physical contact beyond what you've set your standards for, my gifts are nothing but a bribe to fill my own selfish desires.

Real love is patient and kind. Real love is not jealous. Real love is not rude, pushy or proud.

Real love is not easily angered, is not suspicious and does not do wrong.

Real love does not delight in sin or rebellion, but rejoices in truth.

If someone really loves you, he will believe in you, want the best for you and wait patiently for you—and you'll do the same for him.

Real love never fails or gives up. But infatuation passes away, affection weakens because of time and distance, and selfish, false love walks out when the going gets tough.

There are three great virtues: faith, hope and love—but the greatest of these—and the most precious—is love.

Climbing the Ladder

How *can* you avoid trouble when you're on a date? How can you enjoy some physical contact without putting yourself in danger of going too far?

The answer: Stay away from the danger zones on the "Ladder of Passion"—the progression which begins with physical stimulation and ends in full sexual intercourse. Once you progress past a few of the lower rungs, it is very difficult to stop what you and your date have put in motion.

The bottom rung on the ladder is *simple hand-holding*. Hand-holding is nice. It's a sign of affection, and there is nothing wrong with it. But even with hand-holding, the most innocent and simple contact, there is a correct time, place and situation. Hand-holding in an amusement park is great. Hand-holding in church is altogether different — is your mind really on worshiping God or is it on your boyfriend?

The next rung on the ladder is *kissing.* There are kisses on the cheek, on the forehead, on the lips, neck, ears, etc! Each area indicates a different degree of affection. Just be sure the kisses you are giving and receiving agree with your situation. You probably wouldn't want your grandfather to kiss you on the lips; likewise, you wouldn't want your fiancé to always kiss you on the cheek! But I've got to tell you — one of the nicest first dates I ever had didn't end with a kiss, but with a playful tweak of my nose!

Kissing is not required, you know. The thing I used to dread most each time I went out with a guy for the first time was the arrival back at my house. I'd spend the last part of each date worrying about, *Is he going to try to kiss me goodnight? Do I want him to? Should I invite him in or should I go in as soon as possible? If I don't do what he's thinking, will he ever ask me out again?*

By the time I dated Gary, the guy who became my husband, I learned not to expect anything. He wasn't really the mushy romantic type, and when, after four months of dating, he *finally* put his arm around me and began to kiss me, I asked him, "What are you doing?" He just grinned and said, "I'm going to kiss you." I just settled back and decided to enjoy it!

So if you are dating a guy who isn't constantly trying to get physical, enjoy it. It just may be that he has his priorities in order.

But aren't all Christian young men gentlemen? Surely none of them would ever try to get you to do anything wrong!

Don't count on it. As I mentioned earlier, most guys—Christian or not—tend to go up the ladder just as far as the girl will let them go. It isn't right, but it is usually true. So don't think dating a Christian guy is insurance against physical pressure on a date—it may not be.

The next rung on the ladder is *French kissing*. I've heard many people debate French kissing; one youth pastor I know calls it "intercourse above the waist." I can't say if it's wrong or right, but it is a definite progression *up* on the "Ladder of Passion." It may be wise for you to draw the line before this step.

The next rung on the ladder is *fondling*—handling the sexual body parts—*through clothing*. This rung is definitely in the "warning" zone. Usually it is the guy who initiates fondling by placing his hands on a girl's breasts while they are kissing. All a girl has to do is quietly remove his hand and hold it. That will send a message: "I don't want to do this." Send that message several times, and do it verbally if you have to.

The next rung is *fondling with clothes unbuttoned, unzipped or totally removed.* You are definitely in the "danger" zone here, because you are guilty of what some people call "defrauding"—you are arousing desires which cannot rightly be fulfilled. You may have heard guys say of a girl, "She's a tease." No one likes a tease. Guys get tired of that game very quickly. If you lead up to things you can't, or won't, deliver, though, you are guilty of teasing.

Fondling is actually foreplay to sexual intercourse, and if you want to remain morally pure you have no business this far up the ladder.

The next steps up the ladder are *more foreplay to sexual intercourse.* Lying together on a bed, in a car or on a couch is a prelude to intercourse. Allowing a guy to place his fingers or his penis near your vagina is a prelude also, and once he has inserted his penis into your body, you have had sexual intercourse.

If you engage in intercourse before marriage, you have given your most intimate self to someone who may or may not be the person with whom you will want to give your entire life—your husband.

So where do you draw the line? What standards do you set regarding physical affection?

Drawing the Line

We asked our young people what they thought was the farthest physical level a guy and girl could "safely" go on a date. Sixty-one percent listed "kissing/necking/making out"; 20 percent specifically said, "French kissing"; and 15 percent listed touching, embracing or holding hands.

"Kissing *big* time is the limit," wrote one guy.

"*Super* kissing," wrote another.

"Heavy kissing and light touching," wrote a girl.

Before you set your limit in this area, you need to know that guys are *very* different than girls when it comes to what it takes to "turn them on." Young men are sexually aroused very quickly. Once the desire is aroused, it will be very difficult for him to restrain himself. He can't turn himself "on" and "off" at a moment's notice. Therefore, to be safe and smart, don't allow things to become so hot and heavy that your date becomes sexually aroused.

Also keep in mind that physical relationships, like mental relationships, take time to grow. Beware of any guy who expects you to go too far on the first date. Any guy who wants to go straight to "Lovers Lane" is trouble. I saw a movie the other night where two teenagers met each other, exchanged phone numbers, went out on a date and headed straight to a ball park where the girl lost her virginity in the dugout. She didn't even know the guy! Any guy worth loving should care enough to love the real you, not just your body.

I'd suggest that you draw the line somewhere around French kissing. Perhaps you could safely handle more than that once, but there's a "Law of Diminishing Returns" which says you'll be seeking greater and greater pleasure as you continue to date. It's best to keep things slow and easy.

And while you're doing all that kissing, remember that one kiss really is as good as a thousand. The purpose of a kiss is to show affection, and if you really like a guy, one nice kiss can show as much affection as an hour of lip-locking and heavy-breathing.

If your kisses begin to show lust instead of affection, it's time to do something else. Play a game, watch — actually *watch* — television or go for a walk. After all, if you *really* like this guy, what will build your relationship is the time you spend together talking and learning about each other mentally, emotionally and spiritually.

How to Say No

Connie Marshner has given some wonderful "battlefield" advice about how to answer those lines guys often use on girls to get them to give in. Memorize these responses — you may be glad you did.

He says: "You don't know how to have any fun."
You say: "Yes, I do. I've had a great evening. Let's leave it that way, okay?"

He says: "You don't understand. Guys *have* to have sex."
You say: "Nonsense. Nobody ever died of abstinence, and you won't either."

He says: "I love you so much that I want to give you something more."
You say: "Okay, so give me your self-control and let me keep what I cherish — control over my own body."

He says: "Don't you love me?"
You say: "Well, frankly, if you're that kind of person, no I don't."

He says: "Everybody does it, you know."
You say: "I'm not everybody."

He says: "I'll bet you're just scared."
You say: "Of venereal disease and AIDS, yes. Of pregnancy, you bet."

He says: "But I'll take care of you."
You say: "Thanks, but I can take care of myself for now."

He says: "It's only natural."
You say: "So is death, but I don't want to do that either."

He says: "If you loved me, you'd let me."
You say: "If you loved me, you wouldn't ask."[3]

A Serious Matter...

It is important for you to take the "Ladder of Passion" seriously, because many young girls and women find themselves victims of "date rape." *Rape*, simply defined, is when a man has sexual intercourse with a woman *without* her consent.

I'd like to tell you that rape doesn't happen very often, but that's just not true. And more often than not, a woman *knows* the person who raped her. Dr. Joyce Brothers reported in *Parade* magazine that a study of 7,000 students showed that one in four had been raped since the age of fourteen; 90 percent knew the person before he raped them; and 47 percent were raped on first dates or by "romantic acquaintances."[4]

How can you prevent date rape? First, be suspicious if your date tries to control your behavior in any way. A guy who won't respect your choice of what to wear or what to eat won't respect your "no" either.

Second, be very clear in communicating how you feel. If simply removing his hands or saying "no" doesn't make him stop his physical advances, say, "Get away from me. I mean it!" Be careful of sending mixed messages. Don't say "no" and then return to kissing and/or fondling. Your voice may be saying "no," but your actions are saying "yes," and an aroused guy will usually listen to your body.

When dating someone for the first time, suggest a group date. And *never* go somewhere so private that there is no one around should you need help. If your date attempts to overpower you to have sex against your wishes, resist! Scream, kick or struggle if you have to, as long as your life is not in danger.

If you are the victim of rape, please get help. Talk to your parents, your youth pastor, your Sunday school teacher or a trusted adult friend immediately.

How about you? Have you drawn the line so you stay away from the danger zones? Are you willing to make the commitment to limit physical contact?

Hand-holding and kissing are fun — no doubt about it! Just be sure you're ready to handle it.

Think About It...

1. Name some songs or current movies which encourage teenagers to have sex. What is the message they present? That "everybody's doing it" or "sex is nothing but quick fun" or "if you really love someone you'll sleep with them"? Can you think of any songs, movie characters or television shows which encourage teenagers to *wait* for marriage?

2. What stages on the "Ladder of Passion" are in the danger zone? Why?

3. How can a girl or a guy stop a date who is pressing for sexual intercourse or physical involvement beyond what she or he is comfortable with?

4. Why should sex be saved for marriage?

Setting Your Standards

☐ I will try to avoid situations where my date and I could be alone and easily tempted—an empty house, the back seat of a car, etc.

☐ I will decide which rung of the "Ladder of Passion" is my limit, and I will not allow any date to progress past that point.

☐ I will try to keep the growth of physical affection slow in a dating relationship.

☐ My parents and I will agree that if I ask them how to handle a physical problem, they will not become angry at me or my boyfriend, but will give me advice on how to handle the situation.

8

No Standards?
No Guarantees!

I wish we didn't have to include this chapter. I wish that each of you reading this book would just simply say, "I will not have sex before I'm married, and that's that!"

But many of you won't say it. And many of you who will say it may run into difficulty anyway. It's so hard to listen to your head when your heart is turned topsy-turvy by a guy you simply adore. When it feels so good, it's hard to believe it's so wrong.

But have you really thought about what could happen if you have sex outside of marriage? Have you thought about the effects a decision to have sexual intercourse will have not only now, but on the rest of your life? Imagine your worst nightmare — it could come true.

- Your could get pregnant. Instead of going to college, you end up raising a baby.

- The guy you love so much could lose interest in you.

- You could get a venereal disease.

- You could get AIDS.

- You could get pregnant and tear your family apart.

- You could be convinced to marry someone you don't really love.

- You could be divorced before most of your friends are married the first time.

- You could be convinced to have an abortion and end up battling guilt for the rest of your life.

- You could lose all respect for yourself and your boyfriend.

I'm not trying to scare you, but everything listed above has happened to hundreds of girls. *Don't be one of them.*

Choosing Wisely

Recently my pastor, Charlie Martin, spoke to us about making wise decisions.

"Pat Robertson," he said, "made the unwise decision to have sex before marriage and now that fact has been made public and his reputation will suffer as a result.

"Jim Bakker chose to be unfaithful to his wife and his ministry has been severely hurt. Gary Hart will have to admit that his unwise choice of companions cost him a bid for the United States presidency."

The list could go on and on. There are thousands of people whose lives were changed by one simple unwise decision regarding moral purity. Like them, you will live with the decisions you make for the *rest of your life.*

Josh McDowell has estimated that between 55 and 65 percent of *Christian* young people are currently involved in sexual activity. Those young people are making unwise decisions that may haunt them for the rest of their lives. Bill Gothard has found that of the young people who commit suicide, 93 percent were involved in an immoral relationship. For them, sex did not bring happiness, only destruction and hopelessness.

The poll we gave our Christian teenagers indicated that only 75 percent of the group were virgins. What really worried us was that only 65 percent said they wanted to keep their virginity until marriage.

"I may not get married," wrote a seventeen-year-old guy, "and I want to have sex so I will know what it feels like."

"I'm going to remain a virgin because God wants me to," wrote several guys and girls.

One young person had a simple one-word reason for his virginity: "AIDS."

What You Don't Know Can Kill You

More and more, AIDS is becoming a real threat to teenagers. As you probably have heard, AIDS is a disease which kills thousands of people each year by destroying the body's immune system. There is good news and bad news about AIDS. The bad news is that AIDS is rapidly spreading and it *always* kills. The good news is that unless you participate in a sexual act with a carrier of the disease or shoot drugs intravenously, you are not likely to get it.

The message being spread by the experts is that the surest way to prevent the spread of AIDS in the teenage and adult population is restraining from promiscuous sex and drugs. Those are words worth heeding.

Although many people say using a condom will prevent AIDS, there is at least a 10 percent chance of the AIDS virus passing through a condom, just as there is a 10 percent chance of pregnancy. Condoms, which are made of rubber, can leak or tear. Abstinence, which is what God intended for you, is the best way to keep yourself from danger.

Although I'd like you to refrain from premarital sex because of your Christian convictions, if the fear of AIDS is reason enough to keep you morally pure, fine. That fear could very well save your life.

A Word From Your Peers

Recently someone gave me a plain manila envelope. When I opened it, I found a stack of letters written by girls from a home for unwed mothers. Each girl had written on the same theme: "My message to teenagers."

These girls know what can happen when teenagers engage in premarital sex. Listen to them.

Becky

I would like to explain the effects of sexual intercourse before marriage. A relationship usually starts out to be innocent. First you meet someone; he invites you out on a date. He then proceeds to tell you how beautiful you are and may say that he loves you. Now remember, you just met this guy and this is your first date. He takes you home early in order to impress your parents. At the door, he takes your hands and gently kisses you good night. Your heart beats with excitement and almost immediately you are "blindly in love."

As the relationship deepens, you become more serious about each other. He promises to always love you and never to leave you. He even promises to one day marry you. Promises, promises!

That is what happened to me. My boyfriend and I had been dating for almost a year. We, like most other young people, allowed our passion to flare just short of intercourse. One night we did not stop. Immediately I regretted it, and I believe he did too. We both cried and discussed our feelings. He assured me that he loved me and still had respect for me.

As we continued to have intercourse on other dates, my family life suffered. I no longer respected myself. Because of my guilt, I resented any man who touched me, including my own father. I spent more and more time with my boyfriend and less time with my friends. I lost touch with God as well. My life seemed to be worthless.

Suddenly I found myself pregnant. All of the promises my boyfriend made were forgotten. He no longer loved me or cared that I was carrying his child. He wanted me to have an abortion, but never gave me the money that was needed. He finally stopped calling me. I was left to face the problem on my own. I didn't tell my parents until my fourth month. Needless to say, they were shocked and hurt. They had put all of their hopes, dreams and time into me.

An unwed pregnancy is a hard lesson to learn and one you can avoid. I am very sorry I ever lost my virginity. Saying "no" takes little breath, but gives way to a longer, sweeter relationship.

Andrea

One out of every four teenage girls across America today ends up with an unplanned pregnancy. I used to look at this statistic, never dreaming that one day I would become one of those girls.

I had the most perfect relationship with my boyfriend, or so it seemed to me. We dated for months and months and appeared to have it all together. He was a wonderful, loving Christian which was something important to me. But as we became closer and closer and more comfortable with each other, our feelings got more and more out of hand. All my standards for how a relationship should be fell apart. Sex was wrong, but it began to control our relationship. Even though I couldn't see it at the time, I was headed straight for pregnancy.

I never realized that one wrong action of mine could affect so many people. When the news of my pregnancy became known to the members of my family and the family of my boyfriend, the hurt and disappointment were clear. I felt like a failure, not worthy of anything. Everyone had trusted us together and we had blown it. I had never intended or wanted to hurt anyone. What happened to my boyfriend and me was specifically why God ordained sex for marriage.

I had to get away to get my life back on track again. I moved across the world to a maternity home thousands of miles away. That was the hardest, but the best, thing I've ever done for myself.

I hope my story can help you see the cold reality of what sex can result in when you're not married. Virginity is the most pure, precious and beautiful gift God gives to you. You can save it and make sex beautiful once you're married, or you can turn sex around and make it a sinful act. God can give you control.

Debbie

My message to teenagers is always think before you act. I am sure you have heard that a million times before, but I cannot honestly stress enough how important it really is not to rush into anything before you carefully think it through. Do not just think about the good things that could come from your decision. Be realistic and think of the bad things that could happen too. Most important, look to God!

Faith

My message to teenagers would be, "Don't let yourself get caught up in a boy/girl relationship where the girl might get pregnant." Stay away from places and situations that might tempt you to go all the way. I know it's hard, but it's better to be safe than to end up with an unwanted pregnancy.

I know, because I became pregnant. At first I thought about abortion, but when I learned what abortion really was, I knew I could not kill that little person growing inside of me. I was only seventeen when I got pregnant and I knew I was not ready to become a woman, much less a mother. But it seems like you mature overnight. You have the responsibility to make a decision concerning your baby's future. To me, I think it is the hardest decision a young girl could ever make.

Susie

If I had to give a speech to teens, there is one important message I would tell them—think before you act! You have a whole life before you and just by one silly mistake it can all be taken away. Everything totally changes. Not for just a couple of months, but for a lifetime.

If all teens would listen and really learn from other peoples' mistakes, they might not end up having premarital sex. They need to look at people who did get pregnant or who became a father at an early age.

Don't have premarital sex! Your life and other lives around you change so drastically. You aren't the only one going through a lot of pain, anger and confusion. Your parents are too!

Try to have a lot of self-control. Don't let yourself get caught with the wrong people. If your parents try to restrain you from things they think are wrong, please listen to them. They really know what they are talking about. Also, don't let guys use little lines to get you to have sex with them. You don't need to take their bull. Just get yourself out of the situation and stay out of it.

If anything, take some advice from someone who knows and has been there—me. It doesn't pay to have premarital sex. I chose to and now I'm pregnant and away from home.

If I had it to do all over again, I would choose a different route. Always remember to think before you act!

Amy

My message to teenagers would be to think before putting anything in action. Don't let things like drugs, alcohol and sex get in the way. Say "no" when something comes up. Ask yourself one question: "Do I really need this?" Most of the time the answer will probably be "no," but you might let peer pressure get to you.

Next time you have a problem, think about it. Take time

out to look at both the positive and negative sides. Do what is best, not what you want. Believe me, it will save a lot of grief.

Joanne

What is popularity worth to you? This is a question teenagers have to answer. It may be in different experiences, but sooner or later, somehow, you will answer this question.

Everyone wants to be well-liked. Everyone wants to be accepted and to feel secure. But many teenagers think that the best and easiest way is by playing the popularity game.

I used to think, *If I'm popular, I'm important.* But many problems are encountered playing the popularity game. If you want to be in the game, you will most likely have to leave your values behind. You must play by their rules.

My best friend, Paula, was pretty, sweet, smart and had many other good qualities. But she wanted to be popular. She was willing to do just about anything to attain popularity. She had been asked out by a guy who had a bad reputation. He tried to pressure her into having sex, but luckily, she did not give in to this pressure.

You can be popular, but you don't have to play the popularity "game," involving yourself in things you don't really want to be a part of. Just be yourself and be the best you can be. You can be popular for the right reasons. You can be friendly, have a good personality, be kind and helpful to people. You can also respect the rights and feelings of others without compromising your own values.

Priscilla

The first thing I want to say is sex is not a game. I want you to know that if you have sex now, you will regret it later in life. There are real live results that can come from premarital sex. I know.

I'm seventeen years old and for the past three years I have been involved in sex. I thought the same thing everyone else thought: *Not me. I could never get pregnant. And if I did, I would just run out and have an abortion.* So I kept on. Guess what finally happened: I got pregnant.

I never imagined the problems it would cause. My family is being torn apart because my parents want me to place my baby for adoption and I want to keep it. I realize now that this pregnancy has affected more people than just me. My family will never be the same. They say I cannot come home with the baby and I say I won't come home without it. Other members of my family, such as aunts and grandmothers, try to tell me their opinion of what I have done and what I plan to do. It is so hard to keep quiet and not start an argument. It has resulted in some harsh feelings toward some of my relatives.

My final words to teenagers who are involved in sex are, "Please stop." Life is too precious to worry about pregnancy or catching a disease of some sort. Believe me, it's not worth it.

If you don't think you can stop, then get help. There are plenty of places you can go and if you don't think you can tell anyone, go to the Lord and tell Him. If you ask Him to give you the strength to say "no," then He will. He is the one person who will never let you down.

And for those girls and guys who are virgins, it is perfectly all right to be a virgin. I really wish I was. Don't let peer pressure get to you. If other people make fun of you, just tell them this, "I can be like you anytime I want to, but you can never be like me."

Jenny

My message to teenagers is never have sex before marriage. No matter how interested you are to find out what it feels like, just one time will cause you to seek it more and more and then you may wind up pregnant. If the guy tells you he loves you and you are his only girl, don't believe him. When he is not with you, he is probably telling another girl the same thing.

Sex is something that should stay in marriage, not something that you should share with someone who is probably only out for sex. If you continue to do this with someone you are supposedly deeply in love with, you will ruin your reputation.

Believe me, if a guy is in love with you, he will wait and not pressure you. If he won't wait, he only wants to satisfy *his* needs.

Save yourself for your future husband so you will have something special to share. Please do not make the same mistake I did.

Gina

If you are about to start a serious relationship, please stop and listen. Too many teenagers are getting hurt because serious relationships are turning into sexual relationships. I know that some relationships which are serious are not sexual. But if you find yourself heading in that direction, put a stop to it. After experiencing a sexual relationship you will find it almost impossible to be able to break away without being scarred in some way. Many girls think that after they have shared themselves intimately with their boyfriend, a commitment has been made. But it is not true. Many guys (and girls) think of it as "no big deal."

At sixteen I wanted to break away and experience new things after being with the same boy for ten months. I could not do it. Torn between the feeling of wanting to be free and the feeling of obligation toward my boyfriend, I decided to hang on. A month later I became pregnant.

What if you become pregnant? You would be left to face your parents who tried to "tell you so." You may feel depressed, angry, bitter, resentful, scared. You can also say goodbye to fun weekends, dances, school, your prom, graduation and so many other things.

Please take these words seriously. Get your relationships right with your parents, your boyfriend and with God.

Those letters were written from the heart, and for every letter you've read here, there are a thousand other girls and their boyfriends who would tell you the same thing: Set standards and stick to them. Don't give away something precious for a momentary pleasure.

Doing It God's Way

Mike and Paula Walker are the parents of four boys. They aren't fuddy-duddies. They are young and crazy, fun-loving people. Mike and Paula dated, fell in love and waited until marriage before having sex. They know about the benefits of waiting.

"I was able to look at my wife at the marriage altar and truly say that I had waited for her," says Mike. "Your virginity is a one-time gift that you either can or can't give — there's no halfway. Being able to give that gift is the greatest thing in the world.

"Because my wife and I waited, we didn't have to worry about venereal disease, pregnancy outside of marriage, or the trauma of abortion or AIDS.

"There are other benefits too. If you learn self-control before you're married, it's easier to have self-control *after* you're married. Believe it or not, there are many opportunities to be unfaithful to your spouse, and if you have no self-control, you're in trouble.

"Once I was giving a talk on love and sex in a public school and a cocky dude in the back of the room held his hand up and barked, 'Well, what about you? Did you wait?'

"The question caught me by surprise. The teacher's false teeth almost fell out! I hesitated a moment, then I answered. 'I was a twenty-one-year-old virgin when I got married,' I said, 'and if I'd gotten married at twenty-five, I'd have been a twenty-five-year-old virgin.'

"It was by the grace of God that I remained pure. There were times of temptation and times of struggle, but I waited. You can too!

"Decide now to save yourself for marriage. Just make up your mind that you're going to do it God's way."

If you've been working through this book, you may

feel like you've written a list of standards as long as your arm! Don't worry. You don't have to carry a ten-foot checklist with you on your dates.

Jesus said all the rules God made can be summed up in just two statements: Love the Lord your God with all your heart, soul and mind; and love your neighbor as yourself. Likewise, all of the standards we've discussed can be summed up in two simple guidelines: Date only those who know your Savior; and let your behavior on your dates be God-approvable.

Think About It...

1. What theme did the letters from the unwed mothers have in common? If each girl could go back and do something differently, what would it be?

2. How many people are affected by an unmarried girl's pregnancy? What are the effects upon those people?

3. Are the girls who wrote the letters sincere? Can you trust the words of someone who has "been there"? Why?

4. Do you know an unmarried girl who has had a baby or an abortion? Think about her situation. How has her life changed? What does her future hold?

5. Do you intend to wait until marriage before having sex? Why or why not? What reasons did Mike Walker give for waiting? Do they seem like good reasons to you?

6. Can you think of one simple statement that could serve as the ideal standard for every Christian girl? What is it?

9

If You've Already Gone Too Far

A lot of kids believe in God, but just don't think God disapproves of their sex lives." —Will Peyton, high school senior, National Merit semi-finalist[1]

Alyce and Jon had been together almost a year, but it was over. Their last fight had been particularly bitter.

"So that's it? You're going to walk away from all of this?" Jon had asked. "How can you say you love me and sleep with me, then turn around and dump me?"

Alyce realized how far off-track she had gotten in her relationship with Jon and especially in her relationship with God. She knew things needed to change, but she wasn't exactly sure what to do . . .

What happens when a guy and a girl engage in premarital sex? There's the excitement of the pursuit, the physical charge of hormones and the overriding worry you'll be discovered or embarrassed. You may promise each other that it will never happen again, but unless you severely restrict your dating habits or break up, it will become a regular behavior.

"There's a feeling that it's okay for us to have sex because we're educated and know what's going on," a sexually active honors student told her teacher. "We're not going to get pregnant and burden society with unwanted children. We're going to college and have a future. If we do slip up, we'll get an abortion."[2]

Sounds clean and simple, doesn't it? But in real life, we know that abortion is not the answer, children are not simply "unwanted" and education is not a reason or justification for sex.

What *really* happens after a guy and a girl have sex? Among other things, there probably will be depression, a loss of self-respect, guilt and a spiritual decline for the Christian.

Setting Things Straight

But the slate can be wiped clean in God's eyes. The best thing about being a Christian is the forgiveness we have from God. Through forgiveness we are told that our wrongdoings are forgotten and "remembered no more." God forgets when He forgives. There are steps you can take to heal the hurt you may feel inside and right your relationship with God.

The first step is simply to *calm down*. Know that God loves you and will forgive you. Next, be *cleansed*. "If we walk in the light as he is in the light, we have fellowship with one another, and the blood of Jesus, his Son, purifies us from all sin" (1 John 1:7). You can confess your sins, accept responsibility for them and give them freely to God for

His forgiveness.

Next, *clarify* your situation and tell God in what specific area you want to be made right. Is it your dating life? Your personal habits? Wrong desires? Wrong priorities? Don't pray a vague prayer about, "God, please help me live right," but be specific, "God, I've slept with my boyfriend. I know that's wrong, and I need You to help me reset my standards."

After that, *consecrate* your life, your body and your will to God. "Whether we live or die, we belong to the Lord," says the Bible (Romans 14:8). No matter what you do, resolve to belong to the Lord Jesus Christ.

Next, find someone who can *counsel* you and give you wise Christian guidance. *Confide* in someone: a youth pastor, your parents, a counselor. They can help you see more clearly what God can do in your life. God will not leave you helpless or hopeless. He can take your life and make something beautiful, wonderful and incredible out of it.

Finally, *charge!* "I can do all things through Christ who gives me strength," says Philippians 4:13. And you can! Get on with your life and leave the past behind. The Bible promises that God will direct your paths, and paths weren't made for sitting. They were made for walking, running and movin' on! So step out and venture forth in the faith that God will direct you.

Asking Forgiveness of Others

If at all possible, ask forgiveness of the guy you slept with. Let him know that you're not going to become sexually involved again. Explain your reasons (you could start with the many reasons we've talked about in this book). If he really cares for you, he will listen and try to understand. If he cares more for the sexual relationship, he will probably become angry and may walk out of your life. As much as you can, be prepared for his reaction.

Set yourself a new guideline on the "Ladder of Passion." If you and your boyfriend pass this guideline even one more time, I advise you to take time out of that relationship and not see each other for a substantial period of time. For at least a couple of months, stay away from each other. The sexual urge is a great attraction, and when you're in love and your emotions are all confused, you may not be able to resist the temptation again.

If you and your boyfriend cannot break the old habits which inevitably led to intercourse, you may have to break off the relationship completely. Breaking up may seem like a drastic step, but the consequences of *not* breaking up could be life-shattering.

I know one couple who faces this problem. The girl came to me for counseling after she and her boyfriend had slept together. She felt horrible. I advised her to ask forgiveness of her boyfriend and God and take "time off" from the relationship.

She did everything I asked except stay away from her boyfriend. A month later I met her and asked her how things were going. She burst into tears. She was back in the same situation; they had not learned how to stay off the "Ladder of Passion."

In your future dating relationships, take things slowly and steadily, and don't allow the opportunity for temptation. You don't have to confess your past to every date that comes along; the matter is between you and God. Later, if you want to share it with the man who will become your husband, use your own discretion. God's forgiveness will cover your past.

Perhaps the hardest thing of all will be asking your

parents for forgiveness. They love you and will forgive you if you ask them. But no matter how hard they try not to, they'll be a little reluctant to trust you again. Be patient with them and prove yourself worthy of their trust.

If you've blown it, don't ever feel that you are the only person in the world who has goofed up. We have all sinned. Even though I was a virgin when I married, there were times I fell short of my standards and had to ask forgiveness of my dates and God. There are other areas too in which we all fall short. No one is perfect. Don't give up on yourself. There are lots of people who love you and will be there to cheer you on!

Think About It...

1. Can God forgive a girl and a guy who planned an abortion? Does the guy who paid for the abortion need forgiveness too?

2. Does God forgive us even if we don't ask Him for forgiveness? Find some verses in the Bible to support your answer.

3. When you ask forgiveness, you should ask it of as many people as you've hurt. If a girl and guy have intercourse before marriage, of whom should they ask forgiveness?

4. If you were a parent, how would you feel if your son or daughter asked forgiveness for having premarital sex? Would you be as willing to trust your child on a date? What would it take to rebuild that trust?

5. If you've made a mistake, how important is it to forgive yourself? Why?

10

"I Think
I'm Pregnant"

Lori sat on her bedroom floor, unable to hold back the tears. She couldn't believe this was happening to her.

As long as she lives, Lori knows she'll never forget the sickening feeling that hit her when she heard the doctor's words, "You're pregnant . . ."

For the past decade, more than a million American teenage girls have become pregnant each year. About 500,000 teenagers give birth to their babies.[1] Of the remainder of those pregnancies, most end in abortion and a few end in miscarriage.

What choices does a pregnant girl have? Abortion, adoption or parenting: Which option is best?

In the poll we gave to our Christian young people, 35 percent said they would tell their parents right away if they were pregnant, but 60 percent suggested a different

93

course of action:

> "I'd put money in the bank and pray for wisdom."

> "I'd break up the relationship."

> "I'd get married if I was old enough."

> "I'd quit school and try to support the baby."

> "I'd probably put it up for adoption."

> "Suicide."

> "Pray!"

I was surprised, but 6 percent of the young people said they'd opt for abortion. Interestingly enough, however, all of these responses were from guys.

As we discuss the options available to you if you're pregnant, you'll want to ask yourself what role the father of the baby will have in all this. Is he vitally interested and concerned about you and the baby? Has he left you? Is he willing to abide by whatever decision you make? Depending on your particular circumstances, the father may or may not have a lot to say about what happens to the baby.

Abortion

"I couldn't believe I was lying on that table and was actually asking them to kill my baby. To kill it and take it from me like it was something filthy and rotten. But I did it. I did it and it's over. Sometimes I have to keep telling myself that it's over." —a student at Ohio State University[2]

Jane and John had intercourse in the back of his car on Friday night. They hadn't intended to go all the way. Things just got out of hand. *It'll never happen again,* Jane told herself.

On Saturday, Jane's ovary released an egg which was fertilized by a sperm still alive in her reproductive tract. As she started for school on Monday morning, the tiny fertilized egg began traveling through Jane's fallopian tubes and nestled in the walls lining her uterus. Within the baby's cells was all the chromosomal material necessary for it to grow into an infant, a child and, someday, a man.

Jane's life went on as usual. She fought and made up with John, went to school and practiced under the hot sun with the cheerleading squad. Everything was normal and natural.

Two and a half weeks after that Friday night the unborn baby's heart began beating. Six weeks later its tiny brain began to send out electrical impulses. By the time Jane suspected she might be pregnant because her menstrual cycle was two weeks late, her baby had grown to be one-fourth of an inch long. His body was complete, with a brain, eyes, ears, a mouth, kidneys, a liver, stomach, intestines, a spinal cord and a nervous system. In the next fifteen days he would develop a full skeletal system and learn to move his tiny limbs. At two months, the baby would be able to grasp his fingers and toes, swim, hiccup, suck his thumb, and wake and sleep regularly.

John had no idea why Jane was so upset when she met him after school. "I'm pregnant," she blurted out, her face an odd shade of green.

"You're kidding," John replied. "Are you sure?"

"Yes, I'm sure," Jane hissed angrily. "And I'm also sure it's your baby."

John thought a moment. "Well, can't you fix it? I mean, you certainly can't expect me to marry you. I've got a football scholarship to college and my dad would kill me if anything messed up my plans."

"Your plans!" Jane didn't know whether to faint or scratch his eyes out. "I have plans too, you know. I'm getting an abortion, but I'll need some money from you. I figure $100 will cover half the cost."

"Well," he answered unwillingly, "I guess I can scrape some money together. But it will take a few weeks. Just hang on and don't tell anybody."

When John finally came through with his half of the money, Jane was ten weeks pregnant. The abortion clinic arranged to perform a D&C abortion. The doctor inserted a sharp, curved knife into Jane's uterus and literally cut her baby's tiny body into pieces. The attending nurse stood by to reassemble the baby's tiny limbs to make sure the doctor had removed all the "fetal material"—the pieces of her baby's body.

After the operation, Jane lay on the recovery room bed and nervously fingered the thin blanket a nurse had placed over her. None of the clinic workers who had counseled her ever spoke of her *baby.* They had only referred to the "fetus" or "your problem pregnancy." Jane was now rid of the "fetus," but deep inside her heart she knew she had allowed the destruction of a baby. *If I think about it, I'll go crazy,* Jane told herself, so she determined to put the experience behind her.

Annually 30,000 girls less than fourteen years of age become pregnant; adolescent abortions account for one-third of known abortions in America.

Abortion may seem the quickest and easiest way out of an unwanted pregnancy, but that's hardly true. One researcher found that abortion doesn't solve problems between a couple; it only amplifies them. Dr. Vincent Rue, a researcher in Los Angeles, found that 75 percent of unmarried couples broke off their relationship within thirty to ninety days after an abortion.[3]

And now research seems to indicate that the emotional effects of an abortion can last a long time. Experts have coined a new phrase: "PAS." It stands for **P**ost-**A**bortion **S**yndrome, a recognized mental health problem which generally surfaces from five to nine years after a woman has had an abortion.

Dr. Anne Speckhard, a psychologist in Virginia, has found common symptoms that, though they may vary from woman to woman, usually include depression, a preoccupation with pregnancy, irrational fears, suicidal tendencies and psychosomatic illnesses. Furthermore, victims of PAS may have a problem with drugs and alcohol.

Olivia Gans, of American Victims of Abortions, says, "It is quite a number of years after the abortion before a woman feels its effects. Relief is the initial reaction, but it is not a good indicator. The difficulty is that the women don't go back to the place where they had the abortion, so those people [at the abortion clinics] do not see the [other] results [of abortion]."[4]

There are groups to help women who suffer from the effects of abortion. WEBA (Women Exploited by Abortion), Open Arms and Project Rachel are national groups. There are groups organized in several states as well: Conquerors in Minnesota, Abortion Anonymous in New Jersey, and Victims of Choice in California.

If you or a friend is suffering or feeling depressed after an abortion, go to the library and ask the research librarian to help you find a support group in your area. You can write to the Family System Research Center, 5053 S. 12th Street, Arlington, Virginia, 22204. They can put you in touch with someone who can help.

If you should ever become pregnant — whether you

are married or not—never see the child as a problem. God is the Creator of human life, and that child is created in His image. The child is a distinct person, even though you can't see him or her. God has a plan for that baby's life. Abortion is not the answer to any problems your pregnancy might create. It is an old cliché, but it is true—two wrongs don't make a right.

Abortion is not an option for you. Period.

Adoption

I feel particularly strongly about adoption because I am an adoptive parent. When my husband and I learned we could never have biological children of our own, we still desperately wanted to be parents. As I write this, we have two darling adopted children: Taryn, a six-year-old beauty, and Tyler, a whirling bundle of five-year-old energy.

The decision to adopt was easy for us, although we did endure a lot of expense, paperwork, details and months of painful and seemingly endless waiting. An adoption decision, however, is *not* easy for an unmarried mother to make.

Cindee, a teenage mother, writes: "Each year thousands of unborn babies are killed by abortions. Even though you may be dealing with an unwanted pregnancy and a child you're not ready to take care of, there are many couples who cannot have children of their own who *do* want a child and are ready to take care of it. Instead of cutting off that little baby's life, give it a chance to live in a good home where it will be very loved and taken care of. I know it's a hard thing to do. But there *is* a better way for you, your boyfriend and your unborn child."

No one can tell a young woman whether she should make an adoption plan for her child. It is totally between her and God, but there are some important things to consider.

Who will support the baby? If the young woman must find a job and work, who will take care of the baby while she is working? What about the young woman's future education? Few young mothers are able to go to school, care for their babies and work.

I interviewed a young woman who told why she had placed her baby for adoption: "That was God's baby," she said. "I knew that baby needed a mother and a father, and there was no way I could be both. I can't even support myself, so although it hurt, I realized I could never support both of us."

I believe the greatest examples of selfless love are the young girls who love their babies enough to make an adoption plan for the future. I know without a doubt that the greatest joy of my life was seeing my children come off an airplane and hearing a social worker say, "Here's your baby." It doesn't matter that my children don't look like me or did not come from my womb; what does matter is that they are a part of our family and our love.

You need to carefully consider adoption as an option.

Parenting

Nearly every girl who becomes pregnant *wants* to keep her baby, but very few have the emotional, physical or financial resources to provide what is best for the baby and for herself. Of course, many of the teenage girls who become pregnant *do* choose to keep their babies. That decision has to be thought through considerably.

Teenage parenting is usually not successful unless

there is an extended family structure of loving and supportive parents to step in and give a helping hand when necessary. Financial help is almost always needed in some way, and a young parent will need people to go to for emotional support as well.

Choosing to parent is a serious consideration for the father of the baby as well. How involved is the father of your baby going to be in childrearing? The laws are different in each state, and you would do well to consult with a lawyer. In some states if the father is named on the birth certificate, he is liable for child support payments. He also may be entitled to visitation rights and could perhaps file for custody. Is your boyfriend ready to be a father?

Parenting is a difficult challenge, even for the most mature and established parents. I love my children to death, but there are days when I lock myself in the bathroom to find five minutes of quiet and pray that my husband would come home quickly to relieve me. The good days with small children are tiring, and the difficult days when your children are fussy or sick are physically and emotionally draining.

But there are joys in parenting too: teaching your baby, seeing him laugh, watching your toddler count to ten and sing songs. The simple joys of parenting are the best.

If you or one of your friends is ever confronted with the decision to parent, a number of important things must be considered: Are there people other than the mother who can provide financial, emotional and spiritual support? What future goals and plans must the mother postpone or completely give up in order to raise the child? How will this child affect a future marriage?

A girl must also consider the child's interests. Will he or she grow up in an atmosphere of love and support?

Will he know the love of a strong male figure? Will the child know the joy of a Christian home? Will he be taught the things of the Lord? Will staying with you be the best thing for the child?

If you are pregnant, you're faced with some extremely tough choices. But with the support of family and friends, and guidance from God, it's not a hopeless situation. When it comes right down to it, though, the final decision belongs to you, and you must live with the consequences for the rest of your life.

Think About It...

1. Why is abortion not an option for the Christian? When does life begin — inside the womb or outside the womb?

2. What difficulties might face a girl who wishes to make an adoption plan for her baby? How will adoption affect the father of the baby?

3. What considerations must be taken into mind when an unmarried girl wants to raise her baby alone or with the help from the baby's father? What duties and responsibilities should be expected from the child's father?

11

What Guys Do (and Don't) Want From Girls

Boy meets girl.

Girl smiles.

Boy asks for phone number.

Girl gives it to him.

The big date.

Boy picks girl up.

They drive to a secluded spot.

Boy kisses girl.

Girl responds.

They have sexual intercourse.

Boy drops off girl at her house.

"I'll call you tomorrow," he tells her. "But hey—what's your name, anyway?"

Recently I talked to an average teenage boy I'll call Ron. I asked him what he looked for in a date, and he listed his qualifications:

Most important: Physical—
> • good build
> • pretty face
> • good hair
> • stylish clothing

Important: Social—
> • fun to be with
> • loyal
> • popular with others
> • sincere
> • trustworthy

Less Important: Mental—
> • intelligent
> • witty
> • social knowledge

Least Important: Spiritual—
> • doesn't matter much to me

You'll notice that physical considerations are more important than any other area, in Ron's opinion. Let's be honest. Isn't physical appearance what we *all* notice about a person? We notice whether they are heavy or thin, if they are tall or short, and whether or not they have an attractive face.

In the poll we gave our Christian students, though, we learned that guys and girls *don't* think alike when it comes to sizing up members of the opposite sex.

Eighty percent of the girls indicated that a guy's

personality was important; 60 percent said they notice whether or not he's spiritual; and 51 percent said they take into consideration a guy's looks.

On the other hand, only 10 percent of the guys cared if a girl were spiritual; 55 percent wanted a likable personality; 35 percent mentioned a "pretty face"; and 70 percent wanted someone with a "good body."

So whether or not it's fair, until they mature a bit, teenage boys usually form an initial impression of you based on your appearance. If you weren't born with a flawless complexion, great body and delicate features, make the best of what you have!

One teenage girl gave me her best "beauty tip": "Smile and you'll look great. When you look great, you'll feel better. Take pride in your appearance, because your looks say a lot about how you feel about yourself."

A smile can turn anyone into a beauty! Take care of your outward appearance and cultivate a happy attitude. People are always attracted to someone who is happy and confident.

Being a Woman

Years ago, a woman had to act and think and dress in a certain way in order for guys to think she was "feminine." A desirable woman wouldn't whistle, be intelligent or climb trees. Most of all, she could *never* say what she was really thinking.

I watched an old Fred Astaire movie the other night, and a man was giving advice to a lady who wanted to get out of a date. "You could tell him the truth, that you don't care for him," he said, "but no — that would be unfeminine. Tell him instead that you have a headache."

Those days are gone! Today women are encouraged to be honest about their feelings. But many girls are afraid to say what they are *really* feeling because they might lose their boyfriend. Take a piece of advice: If a boy doesn't love you for what you *really* are and what you *really* think, he is not the guy for you! Be true to yourself.

Learn to be open and honest without being blunt. Learn how to be polite and how to carry on an interesting conversation. The old-fashioned virtues of kindness, courtesy and thoughtfulness still translate into popularity. You may not be the life of every party, but everyone likes someone who is nice to be around.

What Guys Want

Girls always want to know how to catch—and keep—a boyfriend. I suppose if there were a magic formula, someone would get rich selling it. There are some things which can help, though.

What do guys want most in a girl? We asked a group of eighteen- to twenty-two-year-old guys what they considered the most important qualities in the girls they dated. They agreed on five qualities an "ideal girl" must have, listed below in order of importance:

1. Christian

2. Honest and sincere

3. Able to talk openly, a good communicator

4. Good self-image

5. Morally pure

These guys also mentioned other qualities they desired in the young women they dated:

"Someone who will fulfill the biblical role of a wife."

"Someone who will be a good mother."

"A sweet spirit."

"Someone who takes good care of themselves."

"Feminine."

"Fun."

"Someone who is content with what they have."

"Someone who is a hard worker."

"Someone with natural, not artificial, beauty."

Did you notice something? Even though 70 percent of the teenage boys said they wanted a girl with a "good body," not one of these older guys mentioned the ol' bod! These guys have matured, and their priorities have shifted considerably! These guys are closer to thinking seriously about marriage and "having a great bod" just doesn't make a marriage last.

Most guys want a girl who really likes them, but respects them enough to allow a certain amount of freedom. Girls who are jealous or clinging or pushy in a relationship will soon find themselves without a boyfriend. Guys like to feel in charge.

You need freedom too. It's no fun having a jealous or possessive boyfriend. Marsha told me about a boy she used to date. He was really nice, but he began to stay at Marsha's house so much she couldn't even find time to wash her hair without him popping his head into the bathroom to see what she was doing! After Marsha told him she didn't want to see him anymore, his moping around made her lose even more respect for him. "It was nice to think he was that crazy about me," Marsha said, "but I could only stand so much. He drove me nuts!"

What Guys Don't Want

What is it that guys *don't* want in a girl? The group of guys we questioned had definite ideas about what they didn't like in a girl:

"Someone who doesn't talk."

"Arrogance, cockiness and pretty girls who are stuck up."

"Insincerity and dishonesty."

"Girls who play mind games."

"Girls who are boring and have no goals."

"Moodiness."

"Girls who don't listen or only talk about themselves."

"Girls who act like what they think you want them to act like, instead of just acting like themselves."

"Girls who get too serious too quickly."

"Girls who fish for compliments (saying, 'I'm on a diet . . .')."

"Girls who use you for material things—they aren't nice until they want something."

"Domineering, impatient girls."

"Girls who always want to know where they stand without ever just standing."

"Girls who wear too much make-up or jewelry."

"Girls who wear skimpy bathing suits, trying to show off their bodies."

"Girls who are smokers or drinkers."

Now, following these lists of "do's" and "don'ts" doesn't automatically guarantee you'll be "Miss Irresistible" with the men. Every guy is different. Just work at being the best *you* you can be!

Making Dating Fun

Recently my husband and I were discussing our dating days, and one thing we both appreciated about the other was our mutual respect and freedom. We made no demands on each other and did not tie each other down with declarations of "I love you" or "I need you" until after we had dated for almost ten months. By the time we knew we really loved each other, we were ready to get married. You see, we were older (I was twenty-two and he was thirty), and we were tired of playing the dating game.

But you can play the game and have lots of fun dating if you plan your date life wisely and well. Stick to the standards you've established and remember the twofold purpose of dating: to get to know people of the opposite sex, and to get to know one particular person of the opposite sex in preparation for engagement and marriage.

By the way, "fun" on a date does *not* equal sex! You can have fun on a date just by

- eating French fries at McDonald's

- sitting and talking on the beach

- climbing a mountain

- tubing down a river

- snorkeling in an ice-cold spring

- gigging frogs in an airboat

- hurling snowballs in a mock fight

- walking through an amusement park

- window shopping at a mall

- gazing at the moon on a church hayride

- singing around a campfire

- popping popcorn with the lid *off* the popper

- caroling in a nursing home

You're not going to marry every person you date, and the guy you're so crazy about right now may not be who you'll be crazy about next year. Date a lot of different people—you'll learn about yourself and you'll learn about other people with different backgrounds and perspectives.

I hate to tell you what may seem like bad news, but even if you're the nicest, most fun, good-looking girl around, there will be weekends when no one asks you out. Even the most popular girls spend an occasional weekend alone. And what may seem like even worse news is that some guys won't ask you out if they know the kind of standards you've set. Two girls recently told me that some of the guys at their Christian school wouldn't ask them out because their "reputation" had spread—they wouldn't "put out" on a date.

If you're going through a "dry spell," you may be tempted to compromise your standards—*don't!* God will honor you for doing what's right. You will find the perfect, uncompromising young man, if it is in God's plan that you marry, and the wait will be well worth it.

Don't become too stressed-out over dating. You'll find someone who would like to go out with you . . . and when you do, have fun with him! If he's attracted to the *real* you, you've found someone pretty special.

Think About It...

1. Joe is a guy you'd really like to get to know better. You aren't in any classes together, but you know he likes art museums and he plays basketball every afternoon in the school gym. You've heard he's a Christian and you're dying to meet him. How do you go about it?

2. A friend of yours, Susan, is the class wallflower. She's quiet, plain, intelligent beyond belief. Although she could be pretty, she just doesn't seem to care about changing. You know she's lonely for some friends, and she's never had a boyfriend. What advice would you give her?

3. Bill has been hanging around lately and you've heard through the grapevine that he really likes you. You like him too. But he seems painfully shy when he's alone with you, although he's the class clown when other people are around. What could you say to bring him out of his shell?

4. Your parents have been watching your relationship with your steady young man develop for four months. Your mom is beginning to feel that you two are spending too much time together. You need to have a heart-to-heart talk. What can you do or say to put your parents at ease?

5. What is the first thing *you* look for in a guy you'd like to date? Are these qualities *really* important?

12

"Me? Think About Marriage?"

Somehow I always knew I'd be married. Although I'm an independent person, I knew I wasn't so independent that I could make it through life without a best friend at my side. Certainly I had Jesus for a best friend, but sometimes we need a hand to hold and an arm to grip — so God created marriage!

I began my hope chest when I was fifteen. The Revere Wear pots and pans I use today were my first hope chest purchase. My friends laughed at me; my relatives scratched their heads; and my mother prayed I wasn't in such a hurry for marriage that I'd get married while I was still a teenager (I didn't).

But there I was — only fifteen and already with a full set of Revere Wear. I was preparing for marriage in the best way I knew how.

Two years later, when I was dating a guy pretty seriously and it looked like we were headed for marriage, I very clearly remember kneeling by my bed and praying for the man I would marry someday. It is strange, but I know I didn't pray for my boyfriend by name—I suppose I realized deep inside that he probably wouldn't be my future husband. I prayed, "Lord, I just ask that You will be with the man You want me to marry someday. If he's not a Christian now, Lord, I pray that You'll draw him close to You. If he is a Christian, let him grow strong in Your Word. Wherever he is, protect him and keep him well."

Years later I found out the year I prayed that prayer was the year my husband did become a Christian. Though it was four years before we even met, God used circumstances in our lives to mold us into the type of people He knew we needed to be.

Although you may not be planning on getting married until you're out of college and/or well-established in a job, you can still begin preparation for marriage now. Start praying about who your life's partner is going to be.

We asked our church's youth group if they ever thought about marriage. Ninety percent said they did, but 90 percent also said they've done nothing to prepare for it.

Ten percent, however, have begun to prepare in various ways:

"I'm trying to decide what qualities I would like to look for in a husband," wrote one fourteen-year-old girl.

"I've decided how many kids I want," wrote a fifteen-year-old.

"I have a way to go before marriage," wrote one girl. "I've decided not to get married until I'm finished with college."

"I'm shopping for women," wrote a sixteen-year-old guy.

"I've babysat and I've taken cooking classes," wrote a fourteen-year-old girl.

How *do* you prepare for marriage? How do you know when you've found the right person to marry? How can you tell if it's the right time to marry?

Finding the Perfect Person

Perhaps you're one of those people who believes there is one perfect man out there for each Christian girl. That isn't really true. First of all, some people are called by God to be single. And, in reality, marriage isn't simply a matter of *finding* the right person; it's a matter of *being* the right person.

I believe if you seek God's best by not lowering your standards, you will find the person with whom you can build a wonderful Christian home. His strengths will cover your weaknesses; your abilities will strengthen his weaknesses.

How can you find God's best for your life? First, you should know God's best is great!

> Trust in the Lord with all your heart and lean not on your own understanding; In all your ways acknowledge him, and he will direct your paths (Proverbs 3:5,6).

If You Trust in the Lord...

Someone once told me that faith is not belief without proof—it is trust without reservation! God has proven Himself to you in the past, so why shouldn't He do good things in your future? Whenever I am trying desperately to trust God for something, I always remember the countless times in the past when He has done more than I ever dared hope or dream. He's a great God, and you can trust Him to bring His best to you in His perfect timing!

And Lean Not on Your Own Understanding...

Don't *lean* on your understanding, but do *use* it! God gave you your brain for a purpose, and He expects you to learn about people and situations. Learn what your strengths and weaknesses are. Learn what it takes to make a good marriage. Learn how to communicate. Learn how to place another person's interests above your own. Marriage is not for the ignorant. It takes brains to find a man you can love, respect and live with.

But don't totally lean, or depend, on your *own* understanding. Read the Bible and find out what God has to say about marriage, leadership and a strong family. As you seek God's best, you will find His will is never contrary to His Word!

In All Your Ways Acknowledge Him...

In everything you do, on every date and in every dating situation, maintain your Christian testimony and your standards. In your manner, your dress, your words and your conduct, acknowledge that Jesus Christ is the Lord of your life.

And He Will Direct Your Paths

Finding God's best is an active pursuit. Don't just sit at home fretting because God's man for you hasn't arrived gift-wrapped on the front porch. Get out and date! Mix in groups of young people, and make friends. If you trust the Lord, lean not on your own understanding and acknowledge Him in all you do, He *will* direct your paths! You will find God's best plan—and the best man—for you.

Finding Perfect Love

How will you know if your love is real? Real love will withstand four tests:

The Test of Time: Did you "grow" into love or "fall" into it? Even if you "fell" into it, has it grown through time, or is the glamour wearing off?

The Test of Separation: Can you be apart and still be in love? When you are away from the strong personality of your boyfriend, do you still feel the same about him? Do you ever have second thoughts when you are away from him?

The Test of Giving: Do you want to give to your boyfriend? I'm not talking about giving sex, but time and energy and attention. Could you give up on an argument? Can you give up your own personal comfort for him? You can give without loving, but you can't love without giving!

The Test of Protection: Do you want to protect your boyfriend's reputation? Does he want to protect yours? Real love wants to protect and shelter.

Real love will be able to pass those four tests with flying colors!

Creating a Family

There are a few decisions you will make in your life which will affect the entire course of your future. At these points, you stand at the crossroads and entire generations of people will be affected because of your decisions.

The three decisions which will have the most

profound influence on you and future generations will be your decisions to select your master, your mate and your mission in life. You probably have already chosen your master—Jesus Christ. If not, why not take a moment right now and commit yourself to Him?

Your mission in life is what God wants you to do in service for Him. As you go through high school and college, you'll find many opportunities to explore different lifetime vocations.

When you choose a mate, you establish a family which will produce children, grandchildren and countless future generations. The blessings or failures of your family will echo through the lives of your descendants. A Christian family is the greatest blessing you can give your children and their children, because not to be taught of God and His movement in the world is to go through life without the facts.

What is a Christian family? Perhaps you came from a home where every Sunday, without fail, everyone got up, dressed and went to Sunday school and church. Perhaps you were saved at an early age and you've never known anything apart from the church and church people. You're accustomed to church, the Bible and prayer, and you have a good idea of what a Christian family is like.

But perhaps you came from a home where Sundays meant sleeping in and the Bible was simply for display on the coffee table. You've accepted Christ, and perhaps others in your family have as well, but you never really grew up knowing what place Christ was to have in the home.

The Bible says a Christian family is led by Christ. The members respect and submit to one another out of love. Children obey and submit to the parents; the wife submits to the husband; and the husband submits to the Lord.

The word *submit* doesn't mean slavery or blind obedience. It is more like a loving allowance. I have met a few Christian girls (and guys!) who are confused on this issue of submission. To be submissive isn't being silent or totally without an opinion, nor does it mean that the wife is inferior or worth less than her husband. And it certainly doesn't give a husband the right to boss his wife around!

The Holy Trinity is composed of three parts—Father, Son and Holy Spirit—and all three parts are equal in power and glory. Yet two of the three, the Son and the Holy Spirit, willingly *submit* to the Father. Together they illustrate the role of submission in the Christian family. The wife and the children are not worth less than the man of the house; they simply submit out of love and obedience. And Christian husbands are to love their wives as they love their own bodies. "After all," we read in Ephesians 5:29, "no one ever hated his own body, but he feeds and cares for it, just as Christ does the church."

When you accept a young man's marriage proposal, you are selecting the father of your future children, your best friend and your spiritual companion.

The Most Important Thing of All

As you begin to prepare for marriage and seek a mate, do you know what the most important thing is you can give the man you marry? Not friendship. Not sex. Not support.

Those things are very important in a marriage, to be sure, but the most important thing you can give the young man you're planning to marry is *respect*. You may date guys who are friendly, gorgeous, spiritual, funny, talented, intelligent, rich, hard-working and sincere. There is certainly nothing wrong with any of those things. But unless you find a man you can *respect* now and forever, those other qualities will fade.

When a man has been through a tough day, he doesn't need someone to mother him. He needs someone who lovingly respects him and lets him know he's made of "the right stuff."

So when you're out there looking for "Mr. Right," fall in love carefully. Find someone with whom you can talk about important things and little things. Find someone with a godly character. Don't measure each guy you date against a "list." Pray for the man you'll marry. Find someone you will love above every other human and everything else but God. Most of all, find someone you respect.

Think About It...

1. When should young people begin preparing for marriage? What sort of preparation should they start with?

2. It has been said that marriage is the most difficult and demanding of human relationships. Why do you think that is? Why is it also the most rewarding?

3. What do men need in marriage? How can their wives make them feel respected?

4. What tests should your love endure before you decide to get married?

5. What is a Christian family? What is each person's responsibility to God and to each other?

6. Have you ever thought that perhaps God wants you to remain single? How can you discover God's will for your life in this area?

13

The Most Important People in Your Dating Life

Dating should be a really fun time in your life. We've talked about standards, physical contact, love, guys, ideas for dates. But have you ever thought about who the most important people are in your dating life? No, it's not your friends and it's not even the guy you're dating! There are two very special people who can help make dating fun — your parents.

If you live in a Christian home with your two *original* parents, have you ever considered how God has blessed you? Not only do you have Christian parents, but you have parents who work at preserving their strong marriage by giving time, energy and love.

If you live with parents who have a successful marriage, count your blessings and thank God. Thank your parents too. They are building a model marriage from which you can learn.

If your parents have been divorced (perhaps you are

not even living with your biological parents), God has placed you where you are for a reason. If you follow God's guidance, He can use your parents and stepparents to mold you into what you need to be. You can learn from your parents' mistakes. (If you are a child of divorce, and you want to know how to make it through this tough time, we've written a book for you: *Mom and Dad Don't Live Together Anymore* published by Here's Life Publishers. It's available at your Christian bookstore.)

You can also learn from your parents' knowledge. They were teenagers once and they know at least something about what growing up is like. True, they don't know what growing up is like in your exact situation, but they have faced situations similar to yours at some point in their lives. Give them some credit for making it through being a teenager!

Talking About the Hard to Talk About

Have your parents called you in for the big "Birds and Bees" talk? You know, the one where they explain how girls menstruate and boys have wet dreams and how babies are made. If they haven't, they may be waiting for you to ask questions about sex.

The poll we gave our students revealed that 60 percent found it difficult to talk to parents about sex, 30 percent found it easy (but these were all girls), and 10 percent found it "sometimes" difficult. Girls generally find it easy to talk to their mothers, and most guys don't like to talk to either parent.

Where do kids learn about sex? In our poll over 98 percent said they learned what they know from their friends or classes at school. Seven percent said they also learned from their parents; 6 percent learned from television or books; and 4 percent learned from the bathroom walls.

You may think you already know all there is to know about sex. You've heard about sex from your friends, from the movies, from health classes, from music and advertisements. But not all of what you've heard is correct.

You need correct information, and the best place to get it is from your parents. Many parents are uncomfortable with talking about sex, though, and they often put it off until they figure their kids have heard everything somewhere else.

So surprise your parents one night and ask a simple, matter-of-fact question about sex. Your practical attitude should put them at ease, and by asking questions you're letting them know that sex, and everything that goes along with it, can't be explained in one talk. Your sexuality is something you grow into, and you're bound to have questions throughout the process.

If your parents actually faint or act repulsed when you ask them about sex, try talking to a youth pastor or the pastor of your church. They can give you honest, scriptural answers for your questions. You deserve the answers—a lot is riding on your future sexual behavior.

Treating Your Parents Right

My teenage friends at the home for unwed mothers had something to say about parents.

Tonya writes, "Obey your parents and listen to what they tell you. Whenever you think they are being overprotective, remember they are really doing what is best for you."

Torrie says, "God gave parents a very special

knowledge no one else has. We teenagers find it very hard to understand parents. We might not always agree eye-to-eye on certain situations, but we should always obey and respect their decisions.

"Parents deserve much more credit than we give them. It's rough being a parent. They already know what it is like to be a teenager, because they were teenagers once. They did not always agree with everything *their* parents demanded, but now that they have kids of their own they can understand why their parents said 'no' on certain occasions. Our parents love us so much they do not want us to make the same mistakes they did.

"Parents are not perfect, but they come pretty close to it in God's eyes. So remember, whenever you are in a situation when your parents have to say 'no,' leave it at that. In time you will understand why and will be very thankful for the knowledge God gave your parents."

Diana writes, "Respect your parents and the rules they have for you. I think back on the times I would lie to my mother and tell her I was going to the movies when I really went out drinking and doing the things she told me were wrong. I didn't realize how bad I was hurting my folks. I didn't get anything out of being rebellious except hurting my parents. They have done so much for me and I turned around and acted like a very inconsiderate teenager.

"If you are lying to your parents and running around with the wrong crowd, you're hurting the people who love you the most. You will end up paying for your rebellious acts. I ended up pregnant. What will happen to you?"

You know that lying to your parents about where you're going and what you're doing is bad news. Sooner or later you'll get caught, and you could end up spending many miserable nights on restriction.

So "big time" lying is out. But what about other kinds of dishonesty?

You may have a good and honest relationship with your parents, but are you always truthful with them? Or is it easier to tell "white lies" to get out of the house, to hang around with certain people or to cover for a friend?

I always tried to be honest with my parents, but I'll never forget one particular time I chose to "alter" the truth. I was on a date with a guy who was so pushy with me that while we were kissing he tore my dress. We stopped making out and I handled the situation with him. But when I got home I couldn't get in the house without my mother seeing the tear in my dress.

My mom liked this guy, and I didn't want to ruin his reputation with her. So when she noticed the awful rip, I simply said, "You know, the seams in this dress are terrible. I just leaned forward too quickly and rrrrip! It tore!"

I lied and I didn't get caught. But years later I told my mother what really happened. She was shocked that such a "fine Christian guy" could have done such a thing. I realized then that if I had told my mother the truth, I could have avoided the troubles I had with the guy after that incident.

I should have stopped dating the guy the night he tore my dress, but I kept seeing him, trying to keep him at arm's length. Finally, the physical pressure he placed on me was too much and we had a messy break-up.

If I had been honest and confided in my mother about what really went on, several things might have happened—

• She could have told me to stop seeing him, and

though I would have been upset, it was what eventually happened anyway.

- My mom could have given me advice on how to avoid those situations that invite physical pressure, like being in a parked car. I could have used that advice.

- I could have kept on seeing the guy, but used some of my mom's wisdom on how to redirect our relationship from a physical emphasis into something more constructive. That dating relationship could have been something much more productive for both of us.

The Bible says, "A lying tongue hates those it hurts, and a flattering mouth works ruin" (Proverbs 26:28). By lying you aren't helping the friend who went where he wasn't supposed to go. A lie won't help the girl you want to protect. A lie won't keep you out of trouble.

So if your dad asks if your date is a gentleman, be honest. If your mom wants to know if you've ever been in a situation where some friends were drinking or smoking pot, tell her. Your parents aren't being nosy. They just want to safeguard a very important person — you.

Parents and Kids

Did you know you can tell a lot about a person by how he treats his parents? They say if you want to know how a young man will treat his wife after he is married, notice how he treats his mother now. Although my husband's mother died just before we were married, I did have the chance to watch them together. She was very ill from cancer, but Gary was loving, devoted and kind to her. He respected both his parents tremendously, and when I married him I was confident that same love and respect would also be a part of our marriage.

The same is true for girls and their parents. Have you ever stopped to think that your boyfriend might be watching how you treat your parents? Does he see you respect and obey your folks, or does he see you malign or mistreat them? What kind of conclusions is he drawing about you when he watches you with your parents?

Daniel was the son of a Christian couple in our church. He was an outstanding young man, a dedicated Christian, intelligent, a good student and conscientious. One afternoon Daniel and his father were having lunch in a restaurant when another man from the church saw them and waved hello. Daniel's dad invited him to join them. After everyone was seated, Daniel's dad casually asked, "Daniel, what would you like for lunch? A cheeseburger?"

"Dad," Daniel muttered, his voice dripping with annoyance, "you know I hate cheeseburgers."

Daniel's father said nothing, although his son had treated him so rudely. The meal was finished and the group left.

A week later Daniel was walking through the halls of his church when he was approached by the man who had joined them for lunch.

"Daniel," the man stopped him, "I just wanted you to know that I've always wanted a son like you. I always thought you were great. But after seeing the hateful way you treated your father the other day, I don't want a son like you anymore. I don't want that quality in any child of mine."

The man walked away, leaving Daniel with his thoughts. An entire lifetime of Daniel's "being a good kid" had been ruined by one angry remark to his father.

Hey, it's normal and natural that you should sometimes get frustrated with your parents. After all, you're growing up and changing every day, and they don't quite know how to treat you. Yesterday you were more of a child than you are today, and tomorrow you will be one step closer to womanhood. Your parents will make mistakes, and they will make you angry. And there will be times when they totally misunderstand you.

But there will also be nights when they sit on the edge of their bed, unable to sleep because you're late and haven't called. All they can think about is a teenager at your high school who was killed in a car accident, and they pray you aren't dead on the road somewhere.

Or perhaps you've been distant lately and your mom worries that somehow it's all her fault.

Perhaps your parents have placed you on restriction, and though you deserve it, they're worried you'll do something stupid in a fit of rebellion, like run away from home or take a handful of pills.

You may think they're overprotective, but they're only watching out for you the best way they know how. They love you and they are doing the best they can.

It was nice to hear from our student poll that most of the kids felt their parents were fair. "I obey what they say, and in return I'm trusted," wrote one guy.

But if they could, many teenagers would change their parents:

"I'd change their money problems."

"I'd make them change their divorce."

"I'd make them friends rather than persons of authority."

"I'd make them stop arguing."

"I'd make my dad be more caring."

"I'd make my dad talk to me more and make my mom a shade less bossy."

"I'd ask them to agree on their decisions for me."

"I'd ask them to lose weight."

"I love my father, but he has been a bad influence on me."

"I'd let them realize I'm growing up."

"I'd want my dad to take charge of giving out punishments."

"I'd want my mom to be more sensitive."

"I'd want them to offer advice, not a lecture."

"I'd want my mom to be less nosy."

"I wouldn't change a thing!"

Parents Are People Too

Whatever we would like to change about our parents, we have to remember that parents are people too. Nobody is perfect. They are parenting on a trial-and-error basis (you will too someday!), and they are bound to make mistakes. God gave you the parents you have for a purpose, even with all their imperfections. He can work through them to mold you into the person you ought to be.

Take a moment to think: What would your parents like to change about you? Your friends? Your clothes? Your boyfriend? Would you be better off if you changed in any of these areas?

Let's learn to work together. Respect and love your parents. They can be the best friends you will ever have as you seek to find your future husband.

In my work with young people, I've met hundreds of parents and I've *never* met anyone who honestly said, "I'm making it a goal to ensure my daughter *never* has *any* fun!" Your parents aren't trying to be spoilsports or to ruin your life. They simply care about you and want to guard and protect you through the risky time of adolescence. Try to understand where they are coming from, and don't be afraid to sit down and *rationally* discuss your dating rules, curfews and standards.

Your mom can help you in your dating life in ways you probably never thought of. She knows all about what it's like to be young—and in love. She knows how it feels to be nervous around a guy you really like, to go out on a first date, and how important it is to look good. Believe it or not, your mom probably charmed quite a few guys when she was young. She met and won the heart of your dad, didn't she? She can give you some good pointers!

Your dad can be a big help too. He knows how guys think. When he sees you in an outfit that's a bit on the sexy side, he thinks "Wow!" and "No guy's going to think that of my daughter" in the same moment. Having your date meet your dad when he comes to pick you up is what my husband calls "very positive intimidation." A guy respects a girl a little more when the image of a proud and protective father is still fresh in his memory.

If you don't have a dad in your home, find another male figure such as your youth pastor or a relative. Suggest to your date that you'd really like him to meet your youth pastor or Uncle Bob. Explain to your substitute father that you'd like to bring your dates to him for his opinion. If this person is anything like my husband (who often serves in this role for the young people he pastors), he will feel as protective of you as he would his own daughter.

Your parents can be your best advantage as you look for guys to date and one super-special guy to marry. Learn to trust them. They've been there.

Think About It...

1. What was the worst fight you've ever had with your parents? How could it have been prevented?

2. Name some ways your parents can help in your dating life.

3. Do you know the story of how your parents met and fell in love? What emotions do you think your mother and father felt at that time? Do you think they're the same or different from your feelings when you are "in love"?

4. Why do parents worry about their kids? Are those worries justified?

5. If you could change your parents, what would you do? What do you think they'd like to change about *you*?

6. Is it easy to talk to your parents about sex or dating? Is there anything you can do to make the discussions easier?

7. If you were a parent, would you let your daughter go out with the guy you'd like to date? Would you want them going to the places you usually go?

8. How can God work through your parents to help your dating life?

A

You Can
Do More Than
"Just Say No"

Perhaps you're getting a lot of pressure from your friends to "go for it" with the person you're dating. Perhaps your friends are asking you to join in things you know are wrong. Maybe, just maybe, you're wanting to go along with them just so they'll quit bugging you about it.

You can stand up to peer pressure! You've probably heard about the "Just Say No" campaign going on around the country. Saying no is great, but there are other things you can say and do as well. Let's join an imaginary couple on their double date with some friends . . .

Susan and Tom are spending an evening with Mike and Julie. They're in Mike's basement playing pool, and Mike has grabbed a six-pack of beer out of his parent's gameroom refrigerator.

"Come on, have one," Mike urges.

"Naw," smiles Tom. "Alcohol throws my pool shot off."

"I can't," says Susan. "If I get caught drinking, I'll

be on restriction for the rest of my life."

"Come on, chickens," says Julie, taking a swig. "No one will find out."

"No, really," says Tom. "Beer has about a million calories, and I've got to make weight for the wrestling team."

Mike holds up the cans again. "You're stupid to pass up this chance."

Susan puts down the pool stick. "I guess Tom and I will just have to go," she says, picking up her coat.

"Oh, all right," says Mike, putting the beer away. "Let's keep playing."

Do you see how Tom and Susan were able to defeat the pressure of their peers? Even without bluntly saying "no," they used four effective tactics:

1. **Humor** — "Alcohol throws my pool shot off."

2. **Name the truthful consequences of the behavior** — "If I get caught drinking, I'll be on restriction the rest of my life."

3. **Offer an excuse** — "Beer has about a million calories, and I've got to make weight for the wrestling team."

4. **Say you'll walk away** — "I guess Tom and I will just have to go."

No matter what the temptation, any of the four methods mentioned above or just saying "no" can work for you. If you're being pressured to do anything against your better judgment, try these tactics.

If you'd like a good Bible study on this subject, check out *Peer Pressure: Standing Up for What You Believe* by Bill Jones (Here's Life Publishers, 1988). It's available at your Christian bookstore.

Notes

Chapter One

1. Jon Bon Jovi quoted in *Research Ministries Report* (Coldwater, MI), p. 3.

Chapter Seven

1. "What's Gone Wrong With Teen Sex?" *People Weekly* (April 13, 1987), p. 112.

2. James Dobson, *Dr. Dobson Answers Your Questions* (Wheaton, IL: Tyndale House Publishers, Inc., 1987), pp. 293-294.

3. Adapted from *Decent Exposure* by Connie Marshner (Brentwood, TN: Wolgemuth & Hyatt, 1988), pp. 177-178.

4. Quoted in *Youthworker Update* (November 1987), p. 2.

Chapter Nine

1. Quoted in "Teens Are Forging Their Own Moral Code," by Patrick Welsh, *St. Petersburg Times* (December 22, 1987), p. 2D.

2. Quoted in "Teens Are Forging Their Own Moral Code," p. 2D.

Chapter Ten

1. "Teen Mothers: A Statistical Profile," *St. Petersburg Times* (September 25, 1988), p. 6F.

2. "What's Gone Wrong With Teen Sex?" *People Weekly* (April 13, 1987), p. 115.

3. Ann Wharton, "Post-Abortion Syndrome," *Fundamentalist Journal* (November 1987), pp. 63-64.

4. Quoted in "Post-Abortion Syndrome," by Ann Wharton, pp. 63-64.